MW00744984

Uncovering Anger
One Layer at a Time

Dr. Sylvia Galvez

Copyright © 2015 Dr. Sylvia Galvez

Book Cover Design by Brandy Anderson II

All rights reserved. No part of this book may be used or
reproduced in any manner whatsoever without written
permission of the Publisher

All rights reserved.

ISBN: 0692564764 (Barcode) (Paperback)

Printed and bound in the United States of America

ISBN-13: 978-0-692-56476-9

Dedication

I dedicate this book to every person who has been carrying past hurt and pain and feels angry toward his or her parents or others. I devote this book to the former clients of Sullivan's Group Home, San Diego, California.

Special thanks to my loving sister, Hortenica Galvez, who courageously fought ovarian cancer. I love and miss you, Tancha!

Another special thanks to my sister-in-law, Edythe Cawthorne, who put up a good fight against pancreatic cancer; and my brother-in-law, John Cawthorne, who died happy.

CONTENTS

ACKNOWLEDGMENTS

I would like to thank my husband, best friend and mentor, Herb Cawthorne, for his love and support through our life journey together. I would like to thank my Heavenly Father who chose me to reach out to trouble youth and young adults who are angry, frustrated, and mad at their parents and others who hurt them. I would like to thank my mother, Josie, my father, Oscar, and my stepmother, Belia. Also my three sons, Marvin, Mario, and Brandy, and my stepchildren, Jon, Elise and Alena Cawthorne, and my three daughters-in-laws, Ana Jacobs, Sharon-Davis Cawthorne, and Tiffany Grubb, all for believing in me and supporting my struggles to get better. I would like to thank my 15 grandchildren who were patient with me through this writing of this book. A shout out to my big brother, Oscar, my little brother, David, my little sister, Rachael, and my stepsister, Diana. To my two sisters-in-laws, Rosa and Lisa Galvez, I love you for taking care of my brothers; and to my sister-in-law and brother-in-law, Elsa and Robert Connor, thank you for your kindness.

A special thanks to my mentor, Dr. Robert Enright, for sharing his life's work on forgiveness education. To the people of the Fourth District in Southeastern, San Diego, California, especially from Emerald Hills, I acknowledge your support and nurturing. I thank the dedicated people of San Diego County's Department of Health and Human Services, Residential Services, and the State of California's Division of Community Care Licensing for all their support and guidance.

I love you all!

PREFACE

There are millions of people in this world who struggle everyday with anger issues that stem from past hurt and pain. Many of them refuse to uncover the source of their anger. This book is about my life, my struggles and my relentless effort to uncover the anger that controlled me for many years. It is also about my dedication to help young girls who were like me, caught in the grip of debilitating bitterness and resentment.

For many, like me, the hurt and pain began at home during childhood. At 10 years old I saw my parents fighting. It happened almost every Saturday night. Witnessing my parents fighting made me angry and I started fighting anybody who looked at me funny in the neighborhood and at school. At 16, I dropped out of high school and had a baby boy and, before I was 21, had two more. I returned to school at 28 and continued until I earned a Master's Degree. I was still angry but education opened my eyes to new opportunities and new ways to channel my energy. I opened group homes for foster girls. They were angry like me. Through working with them on their anger issues, I learned more about my own. Eventually, I learned the power of forgiveness. That's what this book is all about – the journey and importance of forgiveness.

Chapters 1-3 describe my battles with anger, including constant fighting, indifference toward school, and bitterness toward my mom and dad. These chapters reveal the layers of anger that controlled my life well into my twenties. Chapter 4-10 tell the story of the changes in my life and the foster girls in my care. Enrolled in a doctorate program, I discovered the work of Dr. Robert Enright, a renowned scholar on forgiveness education from the University of Wisconsin. In the book, stimulated by Dr. Enright's groundbreaking work, I share my challenges and victories, and those of my girls as well. Together, we embarked on a journey to defeat anger and find peace in the power of forgiveness.

To understand this book, think of the most powerful reference we have today of the beauty of forgiveness. I learned something really important as I watched the aftermath of the Charleston, South Carolina, shooting in 2015. Nine innocent people were killed in a church while they held Bible study and prayed. I saw something great in the way the families and friends of the victims responded to their unspeakable pain and hurt. The image stuck with me — family members, just days after losing loved ones in such a horrible way, standing there in the courtroom and saying, "I forgive you," to the man accused of the killings. There was a grace in their ability to forgive that moved me and helped crystallize the importance of forgiveness as an option to anger in this book.

My foster girls and I embarked on our own journey of forgiveness. You will see how we uncovered the anger one layer at a time and forgave the people who hurt us. And we forgave ourselves! Forgiveness is a powerful tool and we reveal it here as an example of our victory over anger and rage.

I reacted to my parents as a young child. Little did I know then that they were terrific people who worked hard to give their children a better life. In my youth, I misplaced my anger, blaming them in an unfair and unjust manner. They were young, doing the best they could. It took me years to uncover my anger and reunite with my family. That is the ultimate victory!

I hope this book helps you uncover the anger that resides in you, no matter how it is expressed or displayed.

One day, while taking my daily walk, I was in meditative prayer about this book. A white stork flew past and remained in my sight for some time. This was a sign to me – that forgiveness gives our spirits a chance to soar, free from the bondage of anger.

CHAPTER 1

SATURDAY NIGH FIGHT

I was a very angry child growing up! At 10, I remember being awakened in the middle of the night by my mother and father. They argued, yelled and fought every Saturday night. It was traumatizing. Just 10 years old, I didn't understand why or what was going on. All I knew was that it was Saturday night and every Saturday night led to my parents fighting each other

My father was born in Mexico, one of nine. He tells the story of his alienation from his family at the age of 10. He met his father once as a boy. By the time he was 12, he had smuggled himself into the United States on a fishing boat and settled in Indio, California, working in the fields, staying undercover, taking care of himself. He developed the good habits of work and self-sufficiency.

I learned all that later. When I was 10, I just knew about the fighting.

Sometimes the kids got caught in the middle. One Saturday night, I walked into my parent's bedroom and witnessed my dad tossing my mother across room. That's why I hated Saturday nights. I knew what Saturday meant.

Even as a child, I recognized the patterns: sitting in the living room, drinking beer, listening to music, then, all of a sudden, chaos -- yelling, arguing, and physically fighting. It made me so nervous I started biting my nails. I hated the weekends.

One Saturday night, I saw my dad stomping on my mother's face. She was lying on the floor, still fighting him. He had her pinned down with one foot on her body and the other foot stomping her head over and over. She couldn't get up. My mother called the police that night and they took my dad to jail.

The next morning, I noticed my mother's jaw was broken. I was sad and confused. I didn't understand the situation.

My older brother and younger sister stayed in their beds during the commotion. My younger brother and I got out of bed when my parents started fighting. I would position myself between them trying to make them stop. My younger brother jumped on my father's back to get him off my mother.

I never understood why they fought every weekend. During the week they worked. Everything was clam, no problems. Then Saturday came around. I knew I would be traumatized all over again. I was confused because on Sundays we went to Church, like nothing ever happened.

Looking back, I now realize the trauma I experienced as a child. That's when anger formed within me. I didn't even know it. It was like a blood transfusion that changed everything inside me. I learned by example.

Watching my mother and father yell, argue, and fight each other, being traumatized by it, taught me to do the same thing during my childhood and in later relationships.

The anger about all this worked its way inside me, like a second person. Physically fighting became normal to me when I was mad. Anger seemed natural to me and when I was angry nothing could stop me from fighting. I fought everybody, my sisters and brothers, my friends and boyfriends. Fighting fed my anger and gave me power. Anger made me think negatively. I wanted to hurt other people. Anger made me feel offended. It made me want to get even. Anger built up inside of me like a balloon filled with hot air. Stretched to the limits with hot blistering anger, the anger in the balloon sometimes would leak out in small dosages, making my language and interactions mean toward others. Other times the pressure would make it explode, making me turn to physical aggression, especially when someone looked at me funny, or said something I didn't want to hear. Angry feelings produced a powerful negative energy within me that would influence my life for decades.

Ready to Fight

My parents eventually divorced. My dad moved out and my mom continued to work and care for five children. My mother was feisty, smart and religious. She had a high school education, but, when she was young, going to work every day was the most inspiring thing to me. She would work one job, two jobs, and even three jobs to make a life for her kids. I later realized that my work ethic came from my mother. Her spirit said, "Never stop, never quit, never die." Life may have hit her in the face, my dad hit her in the face, and, if she fell down, she never stayed down. She was up the next morning before the sun came up, and off to work. She didn't have to talk to me about work. She showed me.

The divorce made me angrier. What had happened in my household made me mad at everything and everybody. Shortly after the divorce, my mother purchased a home in a predominately black community called Emerald Hills. When we moved in, Emerald Hills was a middle class community. Today, it's considered an "inner-city neighborhood," code for guns, shootings and gangs. We were the only Mexican family in that neighborhood. I came into the neighborhood ready to fight. I made a few friends, the ones I didn't beat up first. The first day of middle school, I stayed to myself, isolated, ready to fight the first one who looked at me crooked or used the wrong tone of voice at me. I made it through the first day and down to the bus stop. One black girl on the sidewalk loudly said, as a statement and a question, "What is that red head white girl doing going to school with us?" In defense of me, another kid screamed out loud, "She's not no white girl, she's Mexican, from the neighborhood." But it was too late.

The burning anger in the balloon burst. I charged the girl who made those unacceptable comments, tackled her like a linebacker, slammed her to the ground, and started to beat the "white girl" out of her. I slugged her face, pulled the braids out of her hair, and pounded her head on the sidewalk over and over again. I hit her so many times so fast she must have thought she was getting beat up by a machine. I don't know if she hit me because I didn't feel anything, except rage. She deserved what she was getting. My anger said, "Get even!" She was bleeding and crying. The next thing I knew someone was pulling me off her. I was still swinging and cursing, "Bitch, I'll kick your ass again if you *ever* say anything to me!" From that point on the black girls in school left me alone.

I remember that first day, but not much else during my middle school years. Anger had set me on a course of nothing but trouble. I was always ready to fight, a big ball of confusion, mad at the world. Learning meant setting aside the anger and allowing well-meaning people to enter my life with positive lessons. That wasn't happening. I don't even remember sitting in a classroom learning anything. I hung out on the school grounds, like a force of wind that would take someone's head off. My school life became nonexistent and home life was still chaotic. While my mother and father were separated and no longer fighting, I became the fighter in my house. I beat up my brother and sister. Sometimes separately, sometimes together. I beat up their friends. I cursed anyone on the block who got in my way. My mother worked all day, two jobs to make ends meet. I was responsible for my younger siblings most of the time. My way of implementing my responsibility was to beat them into line to make them do what I said.

Anger was my partner, my second personality, my bully protector. I was so mad at my parents nothing mattered, especially in school. I didn't care about learning. As I look back, I realize something was protecting me those years. It had to be. I had no fear of getting hurt or meeting my match. I was Hell on Wheels. Anger was an engine making me go 100 miles an hour toward trouble. And, yet, I was learning more than I could have ever known. I learned more each day about the black culture. There was a soul in this community that I embraced. I learned the music. I loved to dance. Before long, I was braiding hair and jive talking. I incorporated the Black English I heard every day. In this community, there was no verb that couldn't be busted. Words that sounded perfectly normal were actually twisted and misused.

You might hear two or three messed up words in one sentence, such as "I don't want to conversate about that; it was a misunderestimate in the first place." I remember the dad of one of my friends coming home with some Chinese food. He said it was "Compound Chicken." I learned later he meant Kung Pao Chicken! It would take years for me to get my subjects and verbs to match! However, there was something about this community that resonated deep inside me. They looked out for each other, with soft spots in their hearts for those who were hurting and traumatized. It was a perfect place for a ball of anger like me. I wasn't the only one carrying an angry burden everywhere I went. I was just the meanest.

Anger's Vacation I

My dad came around once a week to visit my siblings and me. He could barely speak English. He did the best he could. He married a younger woman. That fueled my anger. After all, I didn't have my father and now someone else did. My mom worked all the time. When I did see her, she wasn't nice to me and I certainly was not nice to her. I felt righteous, like I stood on top of my anger and it made me ten feet tall. Mean words exploded out of my mouth whenever anybody, especially my mother, tried to talk to me about my behavior. I was out of control. I ditched school and hung out in the neighborhood. Finally, in desperation, my mother sent me away for the summer to live with her sister in the Bay Area.

I was 12 years old the first time my mother sent me and my little sister to stay with my Aunt Helen for the summer. She lived in Santa Clara, California. She was a Jehovah Witness; you know, the people who knock on your door to talk about Jesus. She wasn't married and went to church just about every day. I was bored to tears. So I volunteered to care for the children in one of the back rooms, while church went on. I taught them arts and crafts. We prayed.

Everything was calm at Aunt Helen's. No arguments! No cursing! No fighting! Saturdays were just Saturdays. Just the night before Sunday. After a few days, I didn't feel the anger. The ever-present hostility that had crept into my blood was no longer living with me, no longer making me mad at every look, offended by every word. I didn't want to curse anybody out or beat up kids I didn't even know.

Hindsight has taught me that the move to Santa Clara was a one-way ticket for *me*, not my anger. The anger was created by the environment – my mom and dad, arguing, cursing, fighting every Saturday night, and kids in the neighborhood calling me a "white girl." Anger was the method by which my personality incorporated the chaos. I realize now the anger was left behind when I went to a new environment – calm, quite, sterile, regimented, and filled with church, church and more church. There was nothing to be angry about. Deep in my soul, I may have understood that anger didn't have to always be my partner, my first responder, and my enforcer.

Anger's Welcome Back

That Fall I flew back home. Guess what was waiting to
greet me at the airport. The spirit I had lived without for three
months was back, almost as soon as I got off the plane. I
slipped back into my angry attitudes as though anger and I had
never been apart. Within less than a day, I slugged my sister so
hard she cried for an hour. I cursed my brother and beat up
two of his friends. My mother had a new boyfriend. That made
me angry. I cursed him out and challenged him to stop me.
School? What school? I didn't put a foot in a classroom. No
teacher was going to tell me what to do. I spent nine months
skipping school, fighting in the neighborhood, cursing at people
I didn't know, and ignoring every plea by my mother to at least
be civil to my brothers and sisters. I was a 100-pound brick wall
of resentment and fury. Near the end of the school year, at
midday, I walked past two girls on the street near a Taco Shop.
One of them said, "Hey, you white bitch, what you doing in this
neighborhood, acting like you so bad?" I started taking off my
earrings and didn't say a word. The only thing she heard from
me was the sound of fists colliding with her face. She slipped
and went down on one knee. In a matter of seconds, I had
reached maximum rage. I continued to beat her up viciously
until my knuckles bled. Her friend must have been so shocked
by my immediate violent reaction she couldn't move to help her
friend fight me.

I never felt even a tinge of remorse or sadness for the girl I
whipped so badly. She called me "white." She called me
"bitch." Saying something like that to someone as angry as I
was meant that she deserved getting her face bloodied and
disfigured. She was saved because somehow she got away and

18

ran. I chased her and her friend home. The neighbors told my brother what happened. He told my mother. That same day, my mother said, "Sylvia, in June, you're going away again for the summer." I thought to myself – just been back home for nine months and now getting shipped off back to the Bay Area!

When I look back at those days, I cringe at the cold indifference that characterized my heart. The anger justified my actions. My actions gave me power. I was a cute 100-pound stick of dynamite. Not only did I not learn anything in school, I didn't learn anything about restraint, self-control, humility or compassion. All that would come later.

Anger's Vacation II

My mother sent me away this time to stay with my Aunt Mary in Oakland, California. I was only 13. Aunt Mary was cool – tall and slim with long brown hair down her back. She loved wearing nice clothes and high heels. Aunt Mary had six kids. She was married to a tall black man who loved her and her children as if they were his own. It seemed like they were the perfect family. They lived in a nice house. Again, for the most part, my anger stayed home in San Diego, as I played with my cousins and went on family outings. I wasn't cursing or fighting, and Aunt Mary allowed me to stay beyond the summer to attend school. Not long after entering school, my anger joined me. Eventually, the anger balloon burst. I attended the local middle school for a month before I started becoming defiant toward my teachers. There was something about authority, especially female authority, that made me see red. Maybe female teachers reminded me of my mom and, by transference, my anger applied to them. Whatever it was, I had a difficult time listening to my teachers. I was downright disrespectful. Even my Aunt Mary couldn't take it. She sent me back home.

Like baggage waiting at the luggage carousel in the airport, I picked up my anger as though nothing positive had happened while I was away. The school year was the same, just another year without any learning in it. How I got promoted to the eighth grade was always curious to me. There must have been some magic in it – leaving the house on the way to school every day but never really going to school at all and still moving to higher grades along with my peers. I was a defiant smart-ass to my teachers. Yet, I was never thrown out of school or picked up by the truant officer when I wasn't in school. Nobody messed with me.

When I was 14, my mother again sent me away for the summer, this time to my Aunt Lola. She also lived in Northern, California, a place called Half Moon Bay. This summer was the best. She had 7 kids, 5 living with her at home. She didn't provide or enforce any structure with her kids, including me. We did what we wanted to do. Now that suited me just fine.

This was Mexican life on steroids. Rice and beans and tortillas. Hard work. Spanish and chopped-up English. No wonder my language was so bad. I had learned Black English mixed with chopped-up English and bits of Spanish. My verbal skills didn't advance, but I was happy as could be. I loved it. There was Mexican music everywhere. It's really funny, but the soulful dance I learned in the black community made me a star when it came to salsa dancing in the Mexican community.

Like all my black friends would've done, I put extra moves on everything and my cousins wanted me to teach them how to dance. I never told them I was just making it up as I went along.

Aunt Lola lived on a large 20-acre ranch with my Uncle Frank. They worked hard caring for the crops and the land. Uncle Frank and Aunt Lola helped manage the company they worked for. You could always see lots of men working the fields, picking flowers, strawberries and corn. There was a large barn that sat on a hill with supplies and packing space. Aunt Lola packed flowers in there sometimes. Maybe 20 or 30 employees worked in the fields, plowing, picking, cleaning the produce for shipment. The employees were like family to Aunt Lola. They reminded me of the black community where I lived. People always laughing, dancing and working hard.

Most of the employees were illegal migrants. They were hard workers. Every once in a while throughout the week the immigration agents, INS police, drove by to inspect the fields. They came speeding up in their green and white vehicles, like GI Joe Jeeps. They'd kicked up dust, drove over rows of crops, and screech their brakes, starting a commotion that scared me at first. It was like chaos unexpectedly appeared. All of a sudden, the music stopped. The laughter went dead. Men who were calmly picking crops suddenly were running in 10 different directions. White men in boots and green uniforms and cowboy hats jumped out of their GI Joe Jeeps and started running after the men who scattered. I had no idea what was going on. Could it have been illegal to pick crops? Were they laughing too much? After seeing a few of these raids, I started to catch on.

Many of the migrant workers had to have green cards or papers that allowed them to work and live in the United States. Some didn't have the right documentation, so when they saw the immigration INS GI Joe Jeeps driving around, they'd took off and ran. Others would hide so they wouldn't be caught. Getting caught meant getting sent back to Mexico. After a while, I caught on to the game. When I noticed the immigration GI Joe Jeeps driving through the ranch, I sometimes pretended that I was an illegal undocumented immigrant. I ran through the fields, screaming out loud "Immigration, INS, immigration is here, run, run, run!" I figured I could distract the guys in green who got out of the INS GI Joe Jeeps by having them chase me. I never understood why these hard working men couldn't stay in United States and work in Half Moon Bay. They never bothered anyone. Seeing one of them get arrested would turn my stomach. They were treated like dogs or like bank robbers and thieves, or like animals with diseases. When the men got caught, they were thrown down, face in the dirt, a foot or a knee on their backs, hands cuffed behind their backs, then dragged to a truck, driven off and sent back to Mexico. About four weeks later, they'd be back, working, laughing in the fields like nothing had ever happened.

Some of my cousins were close to my age. One, Alice, amazed me. She knew how to drive a car at 14! She drove around the ranch or sometimes to the grocery store for her mother. One afternoon, I asked Alice to teach me how to drive. Alice said, "Okay, come on, I'll get my mother's car." Alice drove my Aunt Lola's car on a dirt road behind the large barn. She explained the gas and brake pedals to me.

I figured if she could drive, I could too. I jumped into the
front seat and started driving really slow. I had trouble
steering, since I could barely see over the steering wheel.
After a few minutes, I had the nerve to speed up and drive
down a narrow winding road. I meant to slow down, but I
pushed the gas pedal really hard, instead of the breaks, and ran
into a ditch. We didn't get hurt but the car was stuck in the
ditch. I hit a tree, too. We were both scared and ran back to
the house to ask my cousin, George, to help us get the car out
of the ditch before my Aunt Lola found out. George looked
at the car in the ditch and laughed. We couldn't get it out.
Finally, we told Aunt Lola. I explained that I unintentionally
pushed the gas pedal, instead of the brakes. To my complete
surprise, Aunt Lola wasn't upset. She said, "Chiva, one day
you will have to buy me a car." I promised her I would.
(Chiva is my nickname. It means "goat" in Spanish.) My
Aunt had her employees used a big truck to pull the car out of
the ditch. The front of the car was so damaged it couldn't be
repaired. That was the end driving at 14.

Aunt Lola's house was a place where everyone gathered to
drink beer, listen to music and dance on the weekends.
Some of our older cousins would come by to visit. Tony was
one who liked to party. He told me, Alice and George to walk
with him to the creek. I didn't even know what a "creek" was.
I thought it was some kind of kiddy place. The creek was
behind my Aunt Lola's house, about a half a mile away. It was
actually a rolling raging river, with a beautiful waterfall a short
distance away. The incredible sounds jumped out at me,
continuous crackling, and rushing water splashing against the
shoreline. I had never heard or seen anything like it. Green
shrubs and trees were everywhere. Cousin Tony pulled out a

bag with some green stuff in it. I asked, "What's in the bag?" He said, "Weed." I said, "What?" They laughed. I didn't know what "weed" was. Tony put some weed in a small white piece of paper and rolled it up like a cigar. He called it "a joint," – lit it, smoked it and passed it on. I felt pressured to smoke it, to at least try it, like they were doing. I did. It about choked me. I started coughing uncontrollably. My throat burned and my eyes watered. I didn't like it. More, I enjoyed looking at the green trees, shrubs, small insects, and listening to the waterfall.

Later that day, I heard a weird noise coming from the hills. My Aunt Lola said it was a baby goat in the hills. Later that evening, the goat continued to cry and cry. The sound of the crying changed, from a sad cry to a pained kind of noise. The sound got louder and louder. I went outside to see why. Someone had shot the goat and, it wasn't quite dead, as two men carried it down from the hill toward the house. I felt so sorry for that goat. That next weekend, the goat was cooked over a large fire pit. I couldn't believe my eyes. I was sick to my stomach. All I could remember was the goat crying and crying. I didn't eat any of that goat meat.

I was having so much fun that I didn't want to go home. So that fall semester, my Aunt Lola enrolled me into the local community high school. I could not believe all the white people in that school. There were very few Hispanics. We sat together during lunch. I saw two black kids in the entire high school. I tried really hard in that school because I wanted to stay in Half Moon Bay with my Aunt.

CHAPTER 2

RIGHTEOUS ANGER

One night, my Aunt and I were up late talking about our family history. Aunt Lola told me stories about her and my mom and dad when they were young that really made me mad. I figured that was why they fought so much on Saturdays. I couldn't believe what my Aunt Lola told me. I boiled over with righteous anger. I was fuming with hostility, mixed with embarrassment and rage.

I'm not sure where I got the expectation that my family was, or had to be, perfect. But, later, I came to understand that was one source of my anger. I hated my mother and father fighting. I hated their divorce. The way my anger was processed, I must have thought I was some kind of moral conduit, the protector of the family integrity, the enforcer of good. That gave me the right to have a weapon – anger, super-sized. Everyone in my way had better duck for cover. After listening to Aunt Lola, I was fit to be tied.

The next morning, I called my mother and told her what Aunt Lola said. She denied everything. My mother was so mad at her sister she made me come home that next day. But the anger that met me at the airport this time was more of a monster than ever. I was hurt, confused, in disbelief. I was back home with more resentment. From that point on, I had no respect for my mother or father. I looked at my parents through different lenses. As far as I was concerned, no one in my immediate family knew anything. When I came home from my Aunt Lola's house, I was a completely different teenager. I was even more overwhelmed with anger, hurt, and confusion.

When I got upset with my mother, I would say terribly mean things to her about her past. I would throw things in the house and damage property. I refused to listen to anything she had to say. I had no control over my negative attitudes and behavior. My righteous attitude fed my anger like oxygen feeds a fire. My family probably said, "Well, that's just Sylvia being Sylvia." But, after what Aunt Lola told me, I had new fuel to justify my meanness. Later, my mother said she sent me away for those summers because my behavior was uncontrollable. My mother's three sisters were all different in unique ways. I learned from all of them, good and bad. Two of them were married and they fought their husbands and cursed them out, like my mom did. It just seemed normal to behave in that manner. My mother's oldest sister loved God and was always in church. I am really thankful, looking back, for that experience. My cousin, Tony, educated me about "weed" at 14. I am blessed that I never liked it. I learned from Aunt Lola some of the family secrets. They were topics never to be mentioned in our home. After she told me the secrets, I remember using the knowledge to empower me to be mean to everybody in my family, as though my meanness was the punishment my parents deserved for not being perfect. It would take years for me to realize how ridiculous and unfair my point of view was.

An Experiment with My Dad

That next summer, I went to live with my dad. I was so out of control, an angry 15 year old. With my dad, there was barely any communication. His young wife was nice to me, but I didn't really feel comfortable living there. I could pretty much do what I wanted. I came to realize that freedom was one way to keep my anger at bay. So I kept myself busy during that summer. I enrolled into a summer jobs program for poor kids in the community. I worked as a teacher's aide at a local elementary school. Here I was, someone who never had done anything in school, working with third grade students! Oddly, I loved it. I assisted the teacher in organizing the classroom, playing with the kids, and helping them with their assignments. After that summer, I went back to live with my mother. That fall I started high school.

While living with my dad I used public transportation to get myself to and from work. One day, on the way to work, I meet this tall handsome black guy who was on the bus with me. He introduced himself, saying, "My name's Marvin." We were the same age. I liked the way he dressed – 501 jeans with a crease down the middle, a nice shirt with clean Stacy Adams shoes. Sometimes he wore a black hat with a brim. Marvin had a really nice smile and personality. Up until this point, I hadn't been interested in boys in any romantic way. I was more of a tomboy, one of the "guys" who could play all the sports, hang out, and hold my own in a fight. A brick hit me when I met Marvin. He became my boyfriend that summer. He was really nice to me. We talked on the phone most of the night, mainly regarding our family problems. He was not getting along with his mother. His parents had divorced. He was the only son.

He had three sisters. When we received our paychecks, I spent my money on me and my little sister. Marvin was forced to give his entire paycheck to his mother so she could buy school clothes for his sisters. After that summer, I went back to live with my mother. That fall I started high school.

My anger was sitting inside of me like a time-bomb. I was angry with my parents. Nothing seemed to matter. I didn't know how to fix my relationships with my mom or dad. Neither one talked to me. I didn't know how to reach out to them. I was doing whatever I wanted to do. Nobody wants to confront a little girl who would say just about anything to be hurtful, who was ready to fight in a New York minute. My boyfriend, Marvin, started smoking weed, so I smoked it too, even though I didn't like it. It made me feel like I wasn't in control and that made me nervous. In later years, I realized the feeling from smoking weed back then influenced my attitude toward drugs for the rest of my life. I never liked them and never used them.

High School without Learning

I attended Lincoln High School. Lincoln High was predominately black and Hispanic. Most of the folks I lived around were black, most of my friends were black. I didn't hang out with the Hispanic kids. The Hispanic students didn't like the fact that I associated with the black kids and so they didn't embrace me. But they never messed with me like they did other girls. I had a reputation that went to school before I did. My high school years consisted of hanging out at the local park, sometimes attending class, maybe twice a week, and going to my friends' homes.

One day, walking home from school, the father of one of my friends picked me up, offering a ride back to my house. While in his car, he pulled out a dollar bill, rolled it up so tight it looked like a little straw, then put some white powder on a magazine cover and it snorted into his nose. He pressured me to do the same thing. I didn't want to do it, but I was scared. He showed me how to hold the rolled up dollar bill close to my nose and breathe in hard, so the powder shot up my nostril. Wow! Wow! Never felt anything like   that before! Hitting that stuff made me jittery about what this man might try to do to me while I was in some kind of cocaine La La Land. When we came to a corner, even though it was a couple of blocks away from my house, I said, "I gotta get out right here!" While the car was still moving and before he could say anything, I was out of the car and running home on the sidewalk. My head was spinning, and I felt like the word "stupid" was on a neon sign flashing in my brain every three seconds. By the time I got home, I was a wreck, with no control over what I was doing. It scared me so much that I never did it again. I never told my friend what her dad convinced me to do.

Like most kids in the neighborhood, two of my best friends lived with only their mothers in the home. They smoked weed, their mothers smoked weed, too, and sold it for a living. I just figured that was the way things were. We were good friends, but smoking weed and getting high was not for me. That didn't mean we didn't do other things we were not supposed to do. We were poor teenagers and when we wanted money, we dressed up coffee cans with white paper wrappings that said, "Donations for the Lincoln High

ROTC." With our dressed-up little coffee cans, we knocked on doors. A quarter here, a quarter there, and we had enough money to buy a soda and chips. We did everything together, especially stealing. At the swap meet, we took new jeans into the dressing room, took off our old jeans, put the new ones on, then we covered the new jeans with the old ones. We did that with tops and blouses, even with shoes. We'd just leave the old shoes and walk out with the new ones. That's how we got our clothes for school.

And we fought. Sometimes on the way to school or sometimes coming home. We were like anger walking down the street, ready to fight. Everything happened so quickly. Me and my friends walking one way, another group of girls walking the other way, and, boom, eye contact: "What the fuck are you looking at, you got a problem?" I snatched the girl by her blouse and said, "You staring like you got a problem!" I didn't wait for an answer. I swung from way behind my back and caught her on the side of her jaw. She didn't have a chance. Her eyes nearly popped out of her head, she was so shocked that things had gone from words to wham in so short a time.

My friends jumped the other girls. We swung, pulled hair, scratched and kicked these girls to the ground. We beat them down, bloodied their faces, all because of eye contact. We chased those girls for two blocks, got tired and went home. I think my friends must have been as angry as I was. We never talked about it. But they didn't think there was anything wrong with me going off the hook over nothing. When I started a fight, they'd jump right in. In fact, our bond was stronger after we beat down girls who merely looked at us the wrong way. When we stole something together, we felt closer. I guess that's how gang members feel.

My high school years were horrible, at home and at school. My mother started dating a black man she met on the job. His name was Sam. He was a good person. I wasn't sure what to think at first. One day, I came home from hanging out at night and noticed that Sam had moved into our home. A few days later, a black woman came to our front door and cursed out Sam and my mother. She was mad and mean. Her language was so sincerely violent it made me scared. As bad as I thought I was, I didn't want to tangle with her. I was not sure who she was. I was so mad at my mother because of that incident. I thought, he better not be married. That made me hot!! It fed my anger. Anger standing on the shoulder of righteousness is a dangerous proposition in the hands of a teenager! Sam eventually moved into our home permanently. As time passed, his children started visiting. Eventually, they moved in for a short while. I became angrier about that, so I moved out without saying anything and went to live with my friends. I was gone for a couple of weeks and no one came looking for me. I felt like my mother didn't care. Basically, I did whatever I wanted. After a few weeks, my mother probably thought, "Where's Sylvia?" A light might have gone off in her head. I think she realized I didn't like her boyfriend and his kids living with us. It took a while, but three weeks later she came to my friend's house and took me back home. Actually, I was very surprised to see her. She seemed like she really cared. I went back home with her thatevening.

High school was just a social place to go hangout. I didn't graduate high school. I really never stayed in class or worried about my education. I was too angry about my home situation, I didn't even want to learn. The school system in the late 70s and early 80s passed students to the next grade level no matter how much work they did or didn't do. As long as the student was present in class – sometimes. I think the black and Mexican kids were merely numbers to the school system in my community. In fact, I was surprised I made it out of middle school. I was more shocked the first day I went to Lincoln High School and received a schedule for 10th grade classes. "Tenth grade," I thought, "How did I earn that?" I didn't do any work in middle school. Nevertheless, I was moved to the next grade level no matter what I did in class. Half the time I didn't even attend. I had no interest in school, anyway. Some mornings I left out the front door of my home pretending I was going to school. I hid in the back yard or in the basement until I heard that everyone was gone. I went to hang out with my friends. This was my experience for the first two years of high school, until hanging out took on a whole new meaning.

Before long, hanging out became a code for planning criminal activities. One day, with our parents at work and other kids school, my friends and I broke into a house in the neighborhood. We knew the people who lived there. My friends took things out of the house, but I couldn't do it. My stomach got sick. It was ironic. I could beat down a girl I didn't even know for merely looking at me the wrong way, but breaking into someone's house turned my stomach. I felt this was wrong. In the black community, a lot of kids my age felt that what someone else had could rightfully be theirs if they could get it when the other person wasn't looking or was at work. My friends had no hesitations when it came to stealing stuff out of the houses of people they knew, even friends they had. Hanging out wasn't the same anymore. Instead of listening to music and practicing dance steps, walking around the neighborhood looking for fights, my friends started talking about the next break-in. I learned that I didn't like ripping off the people in my neighborhood. For once in my short life, something moved me to control my behavior. I couldn't tolerate breaking into a home and stealing somebody else's things. I had to figure out a way to get out of this. Going back to Lincoln everyday wasn't an option. So I asked my mother to transfer me to a white school to get away from the peer pressure. She did. Forty-five minutes away from where I lived, Point Loma High School was a totally new experience. It just didn't last long.

CHAPTER 3

PREGNANT AT 16

I continued to see my boyfriend, Marvin, on the weekends and sometimes during the week. He was the one boy who paid attention to me. After all, I was so bad, most the boys were afraid of me. As the stories about my explosive temper got around the neighborhood and the school, boys were careful not to look at me the wrong way, much less in a romantic way. I would whip their asses as quick as I would a girl's. Then I met Marvin on the bus. He didn't know my reputation. He liked me. And since that was new to me, I like it. We talked, day in and day out, until we'd fall asleep on the phone. We talked about getting married, having kids, what we'd name them, getting jobs and buying a house. We laughed, we snuck out at night, and we kissed. It didn't stop there. Before long, I could feel my heart burning to be with him. When I was determined to do something, I would do it. One night, during the week, well after midnight, I grabbed my mother's car keys off the hook by the front door. I tiptoed out and started the car. My only experience driving was crashing my Aunt Lola's car in a ditch and ramming it into a tree. Didn't matter. I was determined to see Marvin. I drove 12 miles on city streets and a short stint on the freeway. Marvin snuck out of his house and met me down the hill.

From there, we drove to a nearby park and made love,

with the backseat flipped down and music on the radio. I had some notion about what we were doing. I had heard my friends talk. I had even seen my cousins having sex under a blanket. I might not have gotten much of an education, but I could add 2 and 2. Marvin was way ahead of me. So I just sat back and enjoyed the ride. Until it hurt. I mean really hurt. I didn't say anything because I didn't know what was supposed to happen. It was strange. It hurt but it didn't hurt. When we were done, about 2 o'clock in the morning, I dropped Marvin off down the hill from his house and drove back home. I felt wetness between my legs like I had to go to the bathroom. I realized I was bleeding on my white shorts. I said, "Oh, Lord, I'm pregnant!" I parked the car, wrapped a sweater around my waist and snuck back into the house. I hung the keys up where they belonged, took a quiet shower, washed my white pants, and went to bed. The next morning I heard my brother, Oscar, joking with my mom about how far from the curb she had parked the car.

Every night, I borrowed the car and met Marvin so we could make love in the back seat. Soon my mother started wondering. She confronted my brother, Oscar, saying, "You been driving my car?" Then she said, "Where's all my gas? I just filled that tank up two days ago!" Within a few days after that, my brother, Oscar, went to the Army. Then my mother really got suspicious. "Somebody out there is stealing my gas!" she said. That night she came home with a lock for the gas tank. I knew the jig was up, the writing was on the wall. I snuck out a couple more times but that was it. Eventually, I had to tell my mother: "It was me who has been borrowing your car at night!"

Marvin may have been ahead of me when it came to sex, but neither of us knew anything about protection. I never learned anything about sex education in school – probably because I never went to school. I don't think any of us learned much about protection in those days. My mother never talked to me about sex or the rhythm method of contraception. As a matter a fact, as a Catholic, my mother would have hit the roof at the thought of talking to her little girl about sex at 15.

One morning, shortly after I had transferred to Point Loma High, I threw up. I felt so badly I couldn't get out of bed to go to school. That was the end of my new high school career and the beginning of my pregnancy with my first child. I still pretended to go to school. I'd leave out the front door each morning and hide in the bushes in the backyard or in the basement until everyone was gone. When everyone left, instead of going to hang out with my friends, I'd creep back in the house and jump in the bed. Sometimes, waiting for them to leave, I threw up in the backyard or in a bucket in the basement. It got so bad I couldn't hide it anymore. When I told Marvin, he was happy. I had to tell my mother.

I threw-up around six o'clock every morning for five months. My mother left to work early in the mornings so she didn't pay much attention to what I was doing. I stayed in bed most of the morning and didn't even keep up my pretense of going to school. I finally told my mother. She said, "I'm taking you to the doctor's office first thing in the morning." My mom's body language told me she was disappointed, although she didn't say it in words. On the way to the doctor's office, she said, "Abortion is against our religion."

I never thought about an abortion anyway. Marvin was
happy, so I was happy. But he was afraid to tell his mother.
He started pretending to go to school, just like I had done for
years. Marvin came by every morning and stayed with me most
of the day. He went home after school hours. His mother
thought he was in school, but he had dropped out.

Anger took a little rest during this time. I didn't go
anywhere. I was stuck at home, so I couldn't get mad at the
way some girl looked at me. Anger did poke its head out from
time to time with my brothers and sisters. Six months pregnant,
me and my brother, David, got into a fight over something. I
turned on the switch and the fury came roaring out. I swung on
him and he swung back. It was bad enough that I had to go to
the hospital, after my mother said, "You better not hurt that
baby!" But everything was okay.

When I stopped throwing-up, Marvin and I started going to
Bible study at a Catholic Church during the week and to Mass
on some Sundays. A religious woman from the church we
called Sister Lisa met with us twice a week. She gave me a small
plaque with an Angel looking over Mary and the baby Jesus.
On it was written,

> The greatest gift that God could send
> He sends with love to you:
> A sweet and helpless little child,
> An obligation, too.
> Each baby that God gives to us
> Is merely lent a while
> To cherish, love, protect, and guard
> From every snare and fall

To form within its childish heart
This image good and true
God bless this new-born baby
And may He bless you too!

That week, I went to confession. I sat in a small space, like a closet separated by a partition, with the priest of the church sitting on one side and me on the other. There was a chair and a wicker square in the center of the partition, like a window with a dark screen between my space and his; but he could see me better than I could see him. I told the priest I had sinned. I was pregnant as a teenager.

He asked one question: "When did this happen?"
Then another, "Was it during the daytime or at night?"
He asked, "Where did you do it?"
I said, "Outside."
"Was this the first boy you've been with in that way?" he asked.
I was starting to feel uncomfortable, but he kept asking.
He said, "If this was the first time, did you hurt yourself?"
Then he asked, "What other things did you do with your body?"
I said, "Nothing."

It was the weirdest feeling. I felt like I was being undressed. I clammed up and gave short one-word answers. The priest told me to do several Our Father prayers and I left out of that confession booth. I've never been in a confession booth since.

On May 6th, 1978, I was getting ready for church, ironing my clothes, when all of a sudden I started having strong back pains. I told my mother and she said, "That's normal." I called my doctor and explained how I was feeling. He told me to get to the hospital and meet him in one hour. I called Marvin and told him to get ready because I was going to pick him up. I was 16 years old, without a driver's license, without a permit. I taught myself how to drive during that year. This time, my mom let me take the car and I picked Marvin up at the bottom of the hill. I drove to Alvarado Hospital and met my doctor in the emergency room. My doctor said I was dilating and in labor and that I was going to have the baby later that night. That was hard to believe because I was only seven months. My doctor instructed me to go to Mercy Hospital. I had to drive another 15 miles, a little scared. I barely felt labor pains as I drove myself to the other hospital.

When I arrived, the nurse assisted in making me comfortable in the labor room. Marvin was with me the entire time. I lay in bed for over six hours, maybe longer. The labor pains escalated to where I had to put the pillow over my face to scream. The doctor finally came in and gave me an epidural shot. The shot reduced the pain. I finally delivered my son, little Marvin. He was 4 pounds, 12 oz. The doctors didn't think he was going to live. I knew in my heart he would. My son had to stay in the hospital for over two months. He had lost 2 pounds. His weight was down to two and half pounds. He stayed in an incubator for seven weeks. The Catholic priest prayed over my baby. The doctors thought he was going to die. Most of every day I stayed in the hospital. For two months, I went home late and returned early the next morning. Sometimes I slept in the hospital overnight. Big Marvin did the same.

He knew he had to tell his mother soon because she thought he was still going to school those days. Big Marvin finally brought his mother to the hospital a few days later to meet me and his son. She was a tall over-weight black woman. She was not happy about the situation. Her energy and body language was rude and mean-spirited. She looked at me, with my baby face and tiny body, and said, "I thought you were an older woman." She didn't even want to hold little Marvin, her own grandson. She was mad and mean. It kind of made sense later. After all, if you've just learned that your only son has given you a new grandson from a young girl you never met, I guess it would make you upset. After the short visit, Big Marvin's mother made him leave with her. Big Marvin didn't come back for a few days. By the time he did, Little Marvin had gained enough weight to come home.

Without knowing it, I learned deep down that there was something sacred about life, the giving of life, and the care of a new born. I went from "nothing matters" to "my baby is the only thing that matters." Sixteen years old, no real education, no means of support, no idea of what was in store, and, yet, a mother with a little baby to protect.

Living on my own at 17 and not a Clue

Seventeen and living in my own apartment! I thought I had arrived. I called this my "playing house stage." I got my own apartment because my mother worked at John Adams Manor. I loved living on my own with my son. Little did I know how challenging being a mother would be.

My anger was still alive and well, but it had to be put in chains for a while. I couldn't walk down the street with Little Marvin a stroller and jump on some girl because she looked at me funny. I couldn't do it, but I wanted to. I would say, "You balled-headed bitch, you lucky I have my son with me or I'd kick your ass right here."

Big Marvin visited us every day. I played house with him too, like I was his wife. Little did I know how challenging being a wife would be. I barely knew how to cook. Big Marvin laughed at me when I tried to cut up a chicken. I am not sure I ever got that right. I sliced that chicken in so many pieces, we had chicken nuggets! My cooking may have lagged, but I was very clean. John Adams Manor was predominately black. My next door neighbor was a black woman whose son was little Marvin's age. They spent the first three years growing up together. I couldn't wait to get my driver's license and buy a car. I hated walking to the grocery store. For extra money, I babysat the apartment manager's kid. I knew how to French braid. I had a steady stream of black girls who wanted their hair in French braids.

I even got into prostitution! Well, not me, not really. My next door neighbor's boyfriend was a pimp. He had several girls prostituting for him. The pimp paid me to do his girls' make-up and French braid their hair. I had to make a living, so I did it. These were real time street-walkers. There was no Internet, no Craig's List hook-ups back then. I would listen to the girls talk about the best corners to pick up Johns and who paid the most. They would talk about sex like it was just brushing their teeth or watching the news. On top of the make-up and hair, I babysat their kids for fifty dollars a night. I made some money, but it wasn't enough.

I went out to look for work. I was 18 years old, so I figured I could find a job. Big Marvin moved in with me when he turned 18. He found a job stocking shelves. Sometimes Marvin Sr. would come by to visit. Grandpa Marvin, we called him. He seemed like a nice cool man. Many times, Big Marvin smoked weed and drank with his father. Back then I thought it was cool. At that time, I never did think about how bad that was for my Little Marvin to see. A grown man smoking weed with his son in front of his grandson. In the future that would be too much generational weed for me. At the time, I was too young to understand how wrong that was!! I still don't know what Marvin Sr. did for a living. He seemed to have a lot of time on his hands. Before long, Big Marvin started to complain about his father's visits. He stayed for long hours throughout that day. Sometimes, Grandpa Marvin had friends meet him at our house. They'd hangout, drink liquor, smoke weed like it was *their* house. I was getting tired of feeling like I was being used or ignored, but, at 18, I really didn't know what to do about it.

Eight months after moving out on my own, I gave birth to Mario, my second son. He was premature too. He had to stay in the hospital for a month. I stayed with him. This time Big Marvin almost never came around to visit. Before long, Big Marvin started coming home late in the night. Sometimes he would not come home for two or three days. I asked him about his whereabouts. He became defensive, avoiding me. I raised my voice. "You're sleeping with somebody!" I would yell. He denied it. But I could smell perfume on him when he came home those late nights. "You got to move out," I said, in not too nice a voice. Marvin was well built, 6 feet, 3 inches, 210 pounds. I was 5 feet, 4 inches, 120 pounds. When he heard me say, "Get out," he grabbed me by the throat and started choking me. I must have passed out because all I remember is I woke up on the kitchen floor. Big Marvin had left.

The next day, I packed up all his belongings and sat them next to the front door. I had the front door locks changed. The next night at about 11 pm he knocked on the front door. I refused to open it. He kicked the door down. He went to my bedroom and didn't see me. He went into Little Marvin's room. That's where he found me. He took his belt off and whipped me over and over again. His eyes looked like he could kill me. I ran through the living room and kitchen trying to get away from him. I tried using the house phone, but Big Marvin grabbed it, pulled the cord out and threw the phone against the wall. Little Marvin was scared, in his bedroom holding his little brother, Mario. I screamed, louder and louder, while I tried to fight him off. Neighbors heard me. There was a knock at the front door. I immediately opened it. It was Virginia, one of the Mexican women who lived a few doors away. She told Big Marvin to stop hitting me. His indifferent evil spirit was distracted for just a second. At that point, I ran out the door to a neighbor's where I called the police. A few minutes later, he was gone. Big Marvin never returned. That was the end of our relationship. I never saw him again and he never saw his boys. The word in the community was that he starting using heroin and never amounted to anything.

I learned that, as a young woman, you're pretty much on your own when a man beats you up. When I called the police on Big Marvin, they didn't do anything. They said they couldn't do anything because they didn't witness the incident. That's how it was in those days. Like they couldn't see the belt marks I had all over my body!

One day, not long after Big Marvin disappeared, a woman came to my front door to look around my apartment. I was on public assistance and she was a representative from the welfare agency. She had a better-than-thou attitude. If looks could say, "I hate you filthy, dirty welfare cheaters," she would have gotten her message across at first glance. It was like she was holding her nose as she approached me. I could feel the disgust and contempt in her spirit. My stomach was already in knots before she said a single word. Two years earlier, her look alone would have prompted me to grab her hair and punch her in the face. That's what she deserved. But I had to bottle up that anger. I used the burning sensation toward this woman to push me forward. Maybe it was my pride, maybe my family work ethic, but, whatever it was, I couldn't stand the thought of this woman seeing me as a cheater, as one who just wanted something for free. Her presence was like being accused of something disgusting that couldn't be proven false. It was a horrible, powerless feeling.

The welfare lady looked around like an investigator with a warrant. Finally, she asked what must have been on her mind the whole time, "You don't have a man living here, do you?" Not many things could make you feel that dirty. The tone sounded like a judge insisting that a criminal was guilty until proven innocent. The "do you?" part was similar to someone threatening, "You better not lie to me!" It made me so mad. I felt violated. I couldn't believe it! I found out that was the rule in the County of San Diego. No man could live in the same house with a woman who received public assistance. My anger was churning underneath. This time, anger put a fire in my soul. It motivated me to go out and find a job. That was easier said than done, given that I had dropped out of high school, and didn't attend much even before I dropped out. Not only did I have very little education, I was ignorant about how things actually worked in the real world.

Every day, I combed the want ads looking for some kind of work I could do. I was so limited. I hadn't studied anything and hadn't really thought about doing anything. The idea of working in an office scared me. Dealing with people made me nervous. When I was younger, nothing mattered. The chip on my shoulder was so big, I looked for reasons to fight, not to learn. True, I had dropped out of high school and didn't have a high school diploma. But, after that welfare investigator agent lady came to my house, with her embarrassing questions and condescending tone, I made a promise to myself that I would always work and never be on any public assistance again. I needed a trade to get off welfare!

I finally discovered a training program to learn the basics of construction. There was no diploma required. Qualifications were more about desire than grade levels. I tried everything – laying bricks, too hard; wood work, too much math; plumbing, too nasty; electrical work, too dangerous. Then, one day, I picked up a paintbrush and a roller and fell in love! This is what I wanted to learn. And I could make money doing it!

For the first time in my life, I started to realize the consequences of squandering my educational chances. I thought to myself, if ever I get the chance to go back to school, I won't waste the opportunities. In the meantime, the training program formed a foundation for me to learn a trade in the construction field.

CHAPTER 4

TIME TO GROW UP

Mr. Willie Davis – oh, what a man! He was a contractor; he became my mentor, a great friend and teacher. Mr. Davis referred to himself as a "tall, dark and handsome kind of guy." I met Mr. Davis through a government program for inter-city youth and young adults. Mr. Davis agreed to mentor me and show me how to become a painter. The paint shop was a place where many of the black contractors in San Diego hung-out. I was the only young woman on the job. I actually looked like a little boy, hair pulled back stuffed in a white hat, a white shirt with white painter pants and work boots – someone had to look closely to identify me as girl.

I felt comfortable. The painters and carpenters embraced me as if I were one of the guys. I loved my first real job! We would meet at the paint shop at seven o'clock every morning to load up the trucks. We worked long hours and fast. Mr. Davis made sure of that. He talked, screamed and yelled a lot, especially when we were moving too slowly or taking long breaks. He never had to yell at me. I worked faster than any of the guys. Mr. Davis and most of the painters smoked cigarettes and that slowed them down. I could do more in an hour than some could do in half a day! I eventually learned how to paint like a professional – it took three years. I learned to paint track homes, small and large buildings, churches, stores, fences, walls, ceilings, and million dollar houses in rich communities.

The guys accepted me, well, for the most part. Sometimes during the week one of them would always say, "You should be home, cooking, taking care of your kids, waiting for your man to come home and chase after you." That advice got stronger the more they noted how well I could work and Mr. Davis kept saying. "Look how Sylvia is doing it!" They hated that. "She shouldn't be doing a man's work anyway," someone said. "Sylvia, go get us some lunch," as though that was all I was worth out here. Another painter told me, "You know, if you was my lady, you wouldn't be out here slingin' paint!" He added, "How you going to catch a man looking like a scrubby painter?" Irritated by all the compliments I was getting for excellent work, one guy expressed how he could get me out of the way, "This ain't no job for a woman, and you need to be home in the kitchen, having babies, not painting buildings!" I just kept painting. The more they talked, the more I wanted to learn the paint trade and beat every one of them on the job. Deep down, although they teased every day, I knew they loved me. Though they said I should get back in the kitchen, I knew that they would take up for me as a painter any day of the week.

I enjoyed painting the homes near the beaches that sat high on the hills, with a view of the ocean. I use to dream about having a home overlooking the water. There was one home in particular that sat high on a hill. From the backyard, you could see the Pacific Ocean extending for miles. The house had enough rooms to get lost. The garage had six spaces with six beautiful cars. One time, during lunch, I stayed inside, walked around and opened a large closet door. There was a beautiful fur coat hanging on a rack. Just looking at it, I concluded, "This woman wears a size 7 like me." That was motivation enough to take the fur coat off the hanger and put it on. It felt good, like I was the lady of the house, a Hollywood star! I dance in front of the mirror for a quick minute and went out to show Mr. Davis and the other painters. I said, "This fur coat is mine now!" It was the first time Mr. Davis really yelled at me. He said, "Go take ass back in the house and hang the coat back up before we end up painting this house for free!" I did a quick little danced move as I turned around to go hang the fur coat back in its place. It was a moment to dream. I loved working with Mr. Davis, but I needed more steady work and benefits. I went to work for the Navy Public Works Center, and continued to work with Mr. Davis on the weekends.

My first paint job for Navy Public Works was on the Marine base in Point Loma, California, painting the exterior of a bowling alley. One day, a young black Marine walked by and said, "Hi." I smiled and waved. My white co-worker pulled me aside and said, "Don't talk to those niggers." I didn't believe what I heard. I could actually visualize myself hitting him in the face with a hammer. Here was a Marine, a young man dressed in our country's finest uniform, prepared to fight and die for this white guy's freedom, and yet he referred to him as "a nigger." It shocked me that he would say such a thing. But he was stuck in his views, like many other white guys on the job. Whenever they saw me talking to black people, they'd call me "nigger lover." I grew up with black people. My best friends were black. My boys were half-black. The black community raised me and nurtured me, even when I was about the meanest, angriest little girl they had ever known. I felt like I wanted to curse out my white co-workers, but I couldn't afford to lose my job. Eventually, I told a black supervisor. I asked if it was okay for me to curse them out. I got my answer when the supervisor moved me to the 32nd Street Naval Station where there was a more diverse community of painters. Problem solved!

The white guys were right about one thing: The black guys were really interested in getting next to me. I was a boy in painter clothes, but when the painter clothes came off, they saw a woman that knocked their socks off. I was petite, with long flowing brown hair down to my waist. My make-up was professional and perfect. I knew how to dress and I knew how to dance. Compared to my painter outfit, it was day and night. By day, a scrubby boyish looking painter who worked on fifty foot ladders and carried five gallon paint buckets without complaint. By night, a hard charging glamorous woman who looked like a million dollars, even if nothing cost anywhere near that much. The Mexicans didn't call me "nigger lover," but they hated the idea that I associated with black men instead of them.

By this time, I had gotten pregnant again with my third child, Brandy. He was named after his father. I was 21, with three kids, with no man worth my weight in cotton. I didn't enjoy being a single mother. It wasn't easy caring for three boys on my own. I got my tubes tied. That was it for me.

Painting allowed me to purchase my first home and a new Toyota car. I was learning what it meant to want more in life. I moved out of the apartments and into a three-bedroom house.

Things were changing in my life. The anger was still there,

just below the surface, but I had responsibilities. Three boys, a job, a house, and a car. It didn't matter that I was just 21. I had work to do and I had better get on with it.

Anger

Painting houses and buildings wasn't going to take me where I wanted and needed to go. Braiding hair and doing make-up as a side business wasn't going to cut it either. I felt deep down it was time to get the education I had thrown away for all those years. I went back to school; first in the community college and then the university. The feeling my first few weeks in the community college must have been what astronauts feel when they lift off above the earth and look back. It was excitement beyond anything I had ever known. I felt out of this world, like I was breathing new air. The air of learning. School looked different and felt different. Remember, it had never mattered before. When I was young, I went to school because I didn't have anywhere else to go. I never went to learn. And now here I was in school, at the community college, feeling like learning was food at a buffet. I couldn't get enough. I was so thrilled by the idea of feeding my brain, I didn't pay much attention to the fact that I was 28 and the students around me were 18, 19, and 20. I didn't notice much about my speech and grammar, as inadequate and unpolished as it was. I was intent on making up for all the time I lost. And I did.

From no high school diploma to an AA Degree to a Master's Degree, I sacrificed and struggled to educate myself and redirect the trajectory of my life.

Five years in higher education enabled a dream to be

planted in my heart. It was a dream about helping traumatized girls who couldn't get past the hurt and pain of life's early experiences. I was in the early stages of recognizing what had happened to me. When I was growing up, there was no one who understood my anger. I thought perhaps I could be the one who understood the anger of the girls I wanted to help. I opened a group home for foster girls whose behavior was too extreme, too violent, too disrespectful, too indifferent, and too dangerous for a normal foster home in the community.

Just like the time the welfare investigator agent lady came to my home and motivated me to get a job, the group home idea was born the same way. Someone told me I couldn't do it, that it was too hard, that the County foster system wanted all proprietors to have a Master's Degree and that I didn't know anything about running a program. The thought of someone telling me I couldn't do something made my anger burn. Sure, I wanted to help girls like me. But, more, I wanted to prove someone wrong – the person who said I couldn't do it.

I got my Master's Degree. I researched how to start a group home. I had never done a proposal for anything, much less a regulated, structured program with money attached that had to be approved by officials. The writing was different than a composition in English class. There were strict guidelines to follow. The language was bureaucratic. I wrote it once. I wrote it twice, then again and again. My grammar was not suited for this kind of writing. My sentence structure was pained and labored, sometimes unintelligible, running on forever. I occasionally put the wrong words in the wrong places. But I kept trying. Finally, I went to the county administration building, looking for guidance. To my great surprise, I discovered that all of the successful proposals were kept in files open to the public. I started reading one, then another and another. After that, I wrote my proposal again. Anger at those who said I couldn't do it wouldn't let me stop. When I submitted the proposal a second time, it was rejected once more. Like a bulldog, I revised it again. And then again. This time, I made it!

I bought a beautiful house on a hill. At the end of a long driveway, it was secluded, with a nice yard and a patio. Two girls to a room. Each girl had a canopy bed, a closet, personal dressers, in a room so nice it shouted, "You are special to me." Many girls came to me with limited underclothes and almost no hygiene supplies. I made sure they had everything they needed. Nevertheless, I had to watch these young women 24-hours a day. There was always staff. But mostly I was there almost every hour of the day in the beginning.

One of my first girls was removed from her home because her great-grandfather had tried to touch her and she told on him. The great-grandfather was notorious. He had molested his daughter, then his granddaughter, and this time his great-granddaughter. But the family was mad at this young girl for telling. She was treated like she was the perpetrator, not the victim. After she was taken away from the family, her mother wouldn't speak to her. The rest of her family treated her like an outcast. They accused her of messing up their so-called happy home. She was consumed with rage over the injustice of it all. The pain showed on her like soot from a fire. The aura around her was dark and mean. She looked out at the world as though every part of it was about to do to her what her family had already done. She was on guard and literally ready to kill.

One day, a week after she had been placed with me, this young girl wanted to hang out with her cousin on a weekend. Because she was so angry and out of control, I had specific instructions not to allow that kind of freedom without the expressed approval of the client's social worker. I had to deny her request. She became very upset. She started by calling me names. She said, "What kind of bitch are you? You have no right to stop me from seeing my cousin, you bitch," her voice got louder. She stormed upstairs. She took the covers off her bed and threw them down the stairs; she pulled out her dresser drawers and flung everything all over her room; she broke the bedroom window. With her bare hand, she grabbed a piece of glass from her broken bedroom window and came back downstairs into my office. I could see death in the stare of her eyes. She charged me with the broken piece of glass in her hand positioned above her head, ready to stab me with it. She held the glass so tightly in her hand blood dripped down her right arm as she came toward me. She was so mad I don't think she could see the blood or feel the pain. She continued to come toward me, with the sharp glass poised to strike. I pushed my chair back, and hurried around my desk. As she tried to swing it at me, I grabbed her right arm tightly and managed to take the glass from her hand. She started pulling my hair. I pushed her back into a chair and then on to the floor. The tension in her body felt like she was made of stone. In a really short moment, she went stiff like a rock, then she began to calm down, all the fight was suddenly gone. The staff member who was in the office with me was shocked by what had happened so quickly. She couldn't move. I yelled at her, "Call for back up!" I held the girl down a minute or two until a male staff member came in to help me. While we were on the floor, the girl started crying. She said, "I hate my mother, my whole family." She said, "They turned on me, they threw me out." Her anger was consuming. She had been the one molested and yet her whole family defended the great-grandfather who molested her. I understood the rage. All I could do at that point was hug her. She calmed down and I let her up off the floor. She was one of the first girls who forced me to witness the outrageous anger that must have been what people saw coming from me when I got mad. This time, I was on the other end.

This incident force me to look back. I realized my anger gave me power like a bully. Other girls would hesitate, if not totally freeze, when my words began to escalate. They could hear the belligerence in my voice and see the meanness in my eyes. The girls I confronted in my early years read my indifference and feared my complete lack of fear. All of a sudden, as a professional working to help girls like me, I was on the other side. Anger burst out *at* me, not *from* me. The anger I had used to give me power was used now to give me pause.

I had one young girl in my care who cried because she never got to know her mother. Her dad was in prison. She was depressed most of the time. She isolated herself from her peers and staff members. She was close to me because I spent quality time with her. I took her to the store to buy hygiene products; I walked with her at the park; I played basketball and softball, always making sure she was picked to be on my team. I sat in her bedroom for several hours a couple of days a week while she played her music and she rocked back and forth on her bed. In rocking back and forth, she was transported to another place, like in a trance. It was her only way to calm down. She said she was lonely. Her extended family had rejected her because she was completely out of control. That's how she ended up in the foster care system in my group home.

While she was in her room, while the music played, while I held her and rocked in rhythm to the music, she was fine. The evening would pass away without incident. But by the next morning, the anger and rage were back. She went to school and everything blew up. A girl started laughing at her, or so she thought. She snapped, "Who the fuck you think you laughin' at?" She never gave the girl a chance to answer. She attacked, stabbing the girl in shoulder just below the neck with a sharpened pencil. The paramedics rush the poor student to the emergency room. My client went to Juvenile Hall. When I went to the school to learn what had happened, I found out the girl who was attacked was actually laughing at a funny comment made by a classmate. My girl had made herself the butt of the joke, when the laughter wasn't in fact about her. "Sound familiar?" were the words that kept bobbing up and down in my head. My stomach burned, when I found out what had happened with this client. She misinterpreted the situation and turned a harmless laugh into a hospital trip for an undeserving classmate. How many times had I done something like that?

It was a wakeup call for me. I realized how many times I had waited for a girl to "look at me funny." I was ready and willing to interpret a glance, a shift of the eyes, a momentary look my way, as an offense, as asking for trouble, as a signal to ignite my rage. It was my reason for taking off my earrings and jumping on an innocent target. Anger wants no dialogue. Anger enables the angry to be judge, jury and executioner without interference from the other person's actual point of view. As a child, I never considered that the justice that came from my fists was unjustified and cruel punishment. I never thought that, maybe, just maybe, the girl didn't mean that glance in an offensive way. Anger has no tolerance for truth. When I went looking for an offence, I asked the question and answered it all in one motion – usually a flying fist to the face.

The effort to help these young girls gave me a new perspective on my own anger. I had to ask myself, "What are you so angry about?" I hadn't been molested. I was never abandoned. I was sent to live with my Aunts but I knew my nasty attitude was the reason I was sent away. So what was it that was tearing me apart at such a young age? Anger made me curse out people. It made me fight. It sucked all the desire to learn out of me. Nothing mattered. Watching the girls in my group home suffer, watching them do the most destructive things possible to ruin their lives, I was forced to look at myself. It was as though I was living in a reality show about anger, with myself and a house full of angry girls as the main characters. Each day, a new script unfolded. And each day I was pushed to the limit to grapple with the utter chaos that anger creates. There was always conflict. Day by day, anger did everything it could to destroy lives.

I was a living example of the adage, "Help yourself by helping others." I had to come to grips with anger, not just to heal myself, but to understand and mediate the power it had over young people. I knew I couldn't help myself if I wasn't honest about the fires of anger that raged in me. The honest reflection about my past helped me understand what my girls were going through. After one of my girls did something really terrible, I had knock-down-drag-out arguments with my staff over whether we should discharge the girl versus taking the extra step to keep her in our care, yet discipline her for acting out her frustrations and anger. The staff always wanted to pounce immediately with the harshest punishment, especially if the anger was aimed in their directions. Sometimes, the staff wanted to "get even" just like the girls did. Perhaps, as a result of my own experience growing up, I always tried to discipline but let go. I tried to dislike the act but not the actor. It was important to keep love alive. The door had to stay open. These girls had been maltreated and that made them angry. They were taken from their homes. That made them angry. The anger made them act out. That pushed everyone away from them. They got punished for acting out. That made them act out even more. I wanted to break the cycle. I tried to clear out my heart so there was always room to let them back in. After a nasty incident, if I saw the smallest positive gesture, I'd give them a smile, a hug, a chance to go out and shop for a pair of jeans or fingernail polish. Most often staff hated it, challenging me by saying, "Why are you rewarding her, the way she acted last night?" They would say, "You're encouraging the negative behavior." Staff rarely saw the glimpses of remorse, the soft words of sorrow, or the tiny gestures that reached out for understanding. But, thank God, I had an uncanny ability to see any positive movement, however small, any opening that allowed us to get past the ugliness of the last episode of anger.

I had the ability to let it go, to forget what the girl had done and move on. That was not only my job, it was my commitment to them. As a result of this ability, I had girls who stayed with me for four or five years, an unprecedented period of time among group home providers. There were girls who ran away and ended up in Juvenile Hall. When their time at Juvenile Hall was up and an opportunity arose to be placed in

another group home, they said, "I want to go back with Sylvia."
If I didn't have an opening, they'd say, "I'll stay in here until I
can go back with her!" They'd rather stay in Juvenile Hall, in
jail, than go somewhere else.

Over the years, there were scores of young girls who lived
at my group home. All of them had difficult circumstances in
their own homes. The removal from their homes was as bad
and traumatic as whatever had happened that caused the
removal. In their pain, I saw my reflection. There was one girl
who was always mad and angry about something. Nothing
seemed to make her happy. She had a chip on her shoulders.
She wasn't friendly to anyone. On a good day, she had a
beautiful smile and could be engaging and pleasant. But most
of the time she wouldn't speak and dared anyone to say
anything to her. Her peers tried to reach out but she refused to
accept their kindness, so they stopped trying. She would say, "I
don't know why no one likes me." She reminded me of me.
The chip on my shoulder was as permanent as a heavy brick and
as light as a feather. It was always there and, yet, it took very
little to blow it off. I had behaved like this young lady behaved.
Everyone stayed away from her. During the holidays –
Thanksgiving, Christmas, and Easter, for example – all the
other girls had permission from their social workers to go on
pass with extended family members. This girl also had
permission too. But she didn't have one family member or a
close friend to take her. No one wanted her. She stayed home
alone with me during those holidays. She cried, depressed,
because no family wanted her. She had a stepsister who lived
around the corner. The stepsister didn't want anything to do
with her. Her negative attitudes and mean spirit caused
everyone to avoid her. She didn't even know what the anger

looked like or where it came from. When I spoke with her about it, she ignored every observation that might have helped her see the damage anger was doing in her life. She blamed everyone but never looked at herself. She did not understand her anger and refused to get help. Observing her attitude and behavior made me realize how ugly I had been. I saw myself in that ugliness.

I wasn't much different than this girl. My family didn't want me around either. Nobody else had a chip on his or her shoulder like I did. I came to a family gathering ready to fight. My aunts and uncles, my cousins and their friends, had to be on the lookout just in case something, anything, made me go off. Most of the time, I fought over the simplest offense. Other times the violation was more serious. Since I lived in a predominately black neighborhood, and most of my friends were black, my cousins might make the dangerous mistake of calling my friends "niggers," or calling me a "nigger lover." In the blink of an eye, the one who said it, boy or girl, would be screaming to my aunts and uncles for help. I might have been a little thing, but I packed a punch. It might take four or five of them to get me off that poor child who opened his or her mouth and let the wrong thing come out. Even as they were pulling me away from my victim, I kicked him or her a couple more times just for good measure. I didn't care if I ruined the whole party. I didn't care if I made family units choose sides. I didn't care if they never invited me back. And they didn't.

In my professional life, as the executive director of group homes for foster girls, I was afforded the opportunity to recognize my own anger by reflecting on the frustrations and acting out behaviors of the girls in my care. I saw myself, when the girls wanted to fight each other because they were mad at the smallest things. I saw myself, when the girls thought someone said something negatively to them and they wanted to fight. I saw myself, when girls angrily said, "She is looking at me in a fucked up way; I want to fight her!" Up until this time, anger was hurting me, killing me, inside and out, and I didn't even know it. I was blind to it. But now I was beginning to understand what had happened to me.

CHAPTER 5

VIEWING ANGER FROM A DISTANCE

I not only achieved a Master's Degree from National University but started to pursue a doctorate from the University of Phoenix. A girl from an inner city neighborhood, a dropout, a teenage single mother – and now a professional with a doctorate! These were achievements of which I could be proud. But until I got a full account of the anger that had controlled so much of my life and found a way to purge it from my soul, I would never feel fully accomplished and free.

This journey helped me view anger from a distance, as though I was looking at myself from a perch on an academic observation deck. Anger was a set of negative feelings that grew inside me like a mental illness. My anger had grown in layers and steps. Anger started taking hold when I saw my parents physically fighting each other every Saturday night. It got worse when they divorced. Anger became part of my personality as a young girl. Anger continued to grow inside me when I had to fight for respect growing up in the neighborhood as a teenager. My angry feelings escalated to another level when I became a teenage mother and was getting beat up by my boys' father. Raising my three boys on my own without support made me angry. My angry emotions were getting worse when my white co-workers were calling me "nigger lover" on the job. During my relationships as a young adult, I was allowing anger to control me. Anger made me fight to get even.

For me, anger *was* a mental illness that hindered my ability to become the individual I was meant to be. Externally, I had beaten some of the odds. An angry dropout who was able to finish school and advance professionally. But anger lurked beneath the surface throughout the journey. Anger made me look for justifications to support my emotional explosions. "It's not my anger that makes me blow up, it's the way I am treated that does it," seemed to be my rationalization. At least, that had been my rationalization for years. I always blamed the girl I beat up. It was her fault she got whacked – "she asked for it!" It took years to learn that angry people blame others, blame everything, but never themselves.

It's a funny thing, but one angry person has an uncanny ability to notice anger in someone else. When the county social workers came to the group home to visit their clients, it was easy for me to identify if they were having a rough day or if they were just angry people who hadn't dealt with their own issues. If they were simply having a bad day, they would usually apologize for their negative tones, short tempers or bad moods. And there were many of them who had a wonderful attitude, real partners in the effort to make the lives of foster girls better. However, for some of them, if the negative aura came from a deeper unaddressed anger, there would be no apologies, no pause to measure how their words and tones affected others.

Working with foster girls created a laboratory of anger. I learned to expect it and work with it. What I didn't expect is that, in working with some of the girls' social workers, I would learn about anger in a totally different light. I learned firsthand how anger in earlier life creeps into professional life and infects decisions – decisions that are supposed to be about the welfare of people end up being distorted to satisfy the anger inside the decision-makers.

I had one social worker who could not rise above the negative behavior of her client, who took everything personally, and mixed her anger into the professional decisions she was supposed to make solely for the welfare of the child. This, of course, made her decisions infected, unprofessional. In one instance, a client in my care had used choice language toward this social worker. She called the social worker, "a bitch," "a fucking liar," and "a Goddamn snitch," all in the same sentence. The social worker escalated her voice in response – something *they* tell *us* never to do. In next few days, the social worker refused to take this girl's calls. She denied every request. If this girl needed permission to take part in a positive school activity, the social worker wouldn't respond, so the girl couldn't take part in it. The social worker allowed her anger to poison her duty as the lead person responsible for this young girl's welfare. And not only that, if anyone tried to moderate her behavior or told her supervisor about her unprofessional attitude, she would go on the warpath against the informer. That's how anger behaves. It does whatever it wants to do and if anyone gets in the way, it treats them as though they were the original offender. The one trying to stop the professional abuse gets abused as though he or she is guilty of a crime. Pretty soon, the room is crowded with offenders. And the social worker is angry at all of them. It's like a toxic waste dump, boiling with anger, making everyone who comes in contact sick and miserable. I saw anger from a distance among the social workers with whom I had to work.

Anger abuses power. In professionals, like some social workers, anger no longer needs a fist, it uses the authority of the office to beat down all offenders and all critics. Professional anger begins with an adult form of what I had come to understand about my anger as a child. Nothing mattered to me at that age. I could beat down a girl and feel nothing for her. Among professionals who have anger churning just below the surface there is a similar feeling – the people around them don't matter. Their feelings don't matter; their thoughts don't matter; their goals and aspirations don't matter. I learned this from one social worker who walked into the group home with exactly that aura of indifference. She made sure everyone knew they were mere bugs who deserved to be stepped on and crushed by the power of her professional standing. If she had been a young girl, her body language, like mine, would have said, "Who the fuck are you looking at?" Instead, as a grown up so-called professional, her body language simply said, "Who the fuck are you!" It was hard to be on a team when the leader of the team thinks you don't matter. I wrote a letter to this social worker's supervisor. After that, she treated me worse. Always undercover, always muted enough to avoid detection, she let her anger about whatever happened to her be the energy that guided her professional interactions and performance.

Angry people often are not conscious of their problems. An annoyed angry person seeks out power struggles, conflicts and constant arguments. I was guilty of that. I'd found fault in others to keep from dealing with faults of my own. I saw that in some of the social workers with whom I dealt. Anger knows no color and does not discriminate. Anger doesn't have an age limit. It forms inside of us as children. If unrecognized and uncovered, anger problems develop in toddlers, continue as boys and girls grow into adolescence, and transform into out of control behaviors in young adults and beyond. In professionals, it operates under the cover of authority. Anger corrupts responsibilities, relationships and marriages.

I have witnessed anger symptoms for many years and have displayed them myself. I remember the physical traits when my anger blew up – red face, tight lips, closed fists, rigid body, hostile posture, and verbal outbursts. This led to physical fights, as well as throwing things and damaging property. Anger creates misery and unhappiness in life, as it did with me. For some the misery and unhappiness causes a turn to drugs and alcohol. Fortunately, I was not one of those.

Suppression of Anger

I discovered that the suppression of anger leads to serious problems, especially if it comes charging out in an area not related to the source of the anger. Suppressed anger is forced down into the recesses of one's soul because something prevents it from emerging. When I was young, nothing stopped my anger from exploding behind a fist against the side of another girl's face. As an adult, the anger couldn't so easily jump out as it did years ago. That didn't mean the anger wasn't there, doing damage like it always did.

During my painting career, when my co-workers called me "nigger lover," I felt what it was like to suppress anger. My stomach was on fire. My eyes saw red. I wanted to fight. The unfairness of their racism made me want to curse them out first, then beat them down like I had done to kids in my youth. In my younger days, an implied criticism would unleash my fury and the person would be sorry forever thinking about me. Now, on the job, they were calling me "nigger lover" and I couldn't do anything about it. I wanted my job. I needed that job. So I pushed the anger down and finished the work day. My rides home were miserable those days. I burned inside, as though the unsatisfied anger punished me for the unwillingness to let it out. When I got home, I was short and grumpy with my boys. Small things set me off. Anger did not get its satisfaction at work and it made me a miserable person at home.

Looking back, it was actually anger that made me lump all my white co-workers together and conclude that they were all "the same way." Anger made me generalize that "white people" called me "nigger lover." It was neat, convenient and useful. It enabled my anger to be fed with prejudice so I could be mad at an entire race of white people for something one or two of them did. It made things simple. These feelings were happening inside me in a quiet pervasive way, and I didn't realize until much later that I was categorizing people just like the ones who called me a "nigger lover."

After opening the group homes, anger had to take a back seat to the goal of serving my girls. I remember a beautiful 16 year old who had a tough go in life. Her Mexican mother was in prison and she never met her black father. Her skin color was dark brown and her hair had tight curls. She spoke fluent Spanish. She was raised by her grandparents, an older Hispanic couple. During Christmas, her family was invited to the group home for a party. When they arrived for the party, her grandparents weren't friendly. They didn't communicate with anyone during the entire party.

The next day, I ask the young girl why her family refused to interact or socialize. She said, "Because they don't like black people!" She added, "They were mad at my social worker for putting me here with black girls." Originally, they had met me, with my light skin and Mexican features. It didn't dawn on them that their granddaughter was going to live in a home filled with black girls and black staff. A couple of days after the party, I received a call from this girl's social worker. The grandmother had complained about her granddaughter living with all these black people. Within days, the county social worker asked her, "You don't like living with all those black girls, do you?" Now the grandmother was bad, but the social worker was worse. It really burned me up and my anger started to boil. Here was a county employee instigating racist feelings and perspectives with her client, a child of only 16. I wanted to kick this woman's ass, but I couldn't. I would have lost not only this girl, but all of my girls. The anger had to be held down or directed in some other way.

Looking back, with the anger being suppressed by my inability to let it loose on the social worker, I can imagine it bursting out elsewhere, like in biting a staff member's head off over nothing or being short with someone in my family. I couldn't let the anger out at that racist social worker, but it had to get satisfaction somewhere. As a result, I was a hurricane with my children. In relationships, I would see something that set me off and my partner wouldn't have a chance. The anger, pent up and shut down in one place, would come barreling out in another. My work with girls who were as troubled as I was began to help me understand the power of my anger, even when I did not let it out in a dramatic physical way.

The best part of it all was that, a short time later, the young girl told her social worker, "It's not bad at all. They're not bad people, and we are the same!" She never let the negative, racist thought in her head. That was a lifetime lesson for me. I noticed that she kept it simple. She didn't throw all people of one race into a large box where she could cover them with prejudiced perspectives and just leave it at that. She saw in them the same qualities she recognized in herself. The empathy was built into her system. I learned from the purity of her view.

A mother of one of my girls came to visit the group home one day. The mother and her daughter were white. When the mother saw the young girl's living environment, she hit the roof. The thought of her daughter living with black girls made her turn beet red with anger. And, then, she found out her daughter was going to go to school with black kids. If she could have turned any redder, she would have. This woman had lost her child for insufficiencies as a parent. She had allowed things to happen to her child that were neglectful, if not criminal. The public system had decided that society was better off if her daughter was removed from this woman's care. In the beginning, she wasn't allowed to see her daughter without someone else present. The state concluded that her daughter was unsafe in her custody. And, yet, here she was spewing foul language and threats about her daughter living with black girls, as though her daughter needed urgent protection from such a terrible danger. And, of course, that included, according to her mother, the "unspeakable dangers" of attending school with these same black people.

There was something about this kind of injustice that made my anger want to emerge as a defender of truth and right. My anger never heard of the notion that two wrongs don't make a right. I wanted to curse her out louder and with worse language than she used. I wanted to beat her until she melted into the ground and disappeared. With my anger leading, I thought, "How can this low-life, racist, hypocritical, superior-acting, incompetent white parent question the quality of a whole race of people in front of these innocent girls who haven't done anything to her?" If she didn't deserve a beat down, who did? But I could do nothing like that. So I herded the girls in the back family room, including the mother's daughter, and went back to escort the mother off the property. My hands were shaking, tears came from my eyes, as I told the mother, "I don't ever want to see you on this property ever again."

Here was another chance for my anger to lump a race of people into a single box, where my opinions about this racist woman could be spread over the entire race of white folks. The infection of group prejudice happened so fast I didn't even know where it came from. Next thing I knew, the feeling I had in my stomach about this nutty woman came charging up when I ran into almost any white person. My anger gave me a right to hold all white people accountable for the few who offended me. It was a slippery slope, with ignorant prejudice waiting at the bottom. My anger encouraged me to say about the mother, "It's because she's white and thinks she's better than me," as opposed to my better side saying, "It's because she ignorant and doesn't know any better."

The mother attempted to get a restraining order against me, forbidding the enrollment of her daughter in a high school with a high percentage of blacks and Hispanic students. She was never granted a restraining order. But the mother's influence was not without consequences. One afternoon, as her daughter mopped the kitchen floor in the group home, a house-mate walked over the area she had just mopped. The daughter became upset and, almost out of instinct, blurted out, "Nigger, you steppin' on the floor I just mopped!" A quiet afternoon turned ugly. The daughter got rushed by the house-mate she called a "nigger," and the battle was on to break it up and keep the peace. Unlike her mother, the daughter had the compassion and good sense to apologize.

As time passed, the daughter liked her house-mates and flourished at school. The daughter lived in our group home for two years and has never missed an opportunity to join us whenever we have a reunion. This young lady had anger all around her, but she manage to look at people as individuals and treat them like she wanted to be treated. I learned a lot from her.

Anger results in negative consequences mentally and physically, such as hopelessness, post-traumatic stress, high-blood pressure, and tension that can create interference with daily living. Anger is closely related to hostility and aggression. The three terms are connected and overlapping, according to Vecchio and O' Leary (2004), in the following manner: anger is an emotion, hostility is an attitude, and aggression is behavior. Deffenbacher (1996) describes two levels of anger, the low and the high.

The low-level anger trait is most often displayed by individuals with low self-esteem, suppressed outrage, insufficient coping skills, tendencies toward drugs and alcohol abuse. The high-level anger trait is more volatile, involving tendencies to blame others and a refusal to allow the anger to dissipate. The high-level anger trait often translates into arguments, aggressive interactions, and physical violence.

CHAPTER 6

STUCK ON ANGER

It took all these years and many experiences to understand the meaning of anger and how anyone can get stuck there. In my life, from the early days, anger built a fort around me from which I could not escape. As I grew, new encounters contributed to my isolation in anger and forced every experience to pass through these feelings of displeasure that were trapped inside me. I missed the enjoyment of growing up with my brothers and sisters because I was always mad and ready to fight. School was never fun, no happiness playing at recess, no laughter in the locker rooms after gym, no rejoicing with teammates after winning a game. There was no happiness in completing a school assignment, no applause from the audience at a school assembly, no teacher remembered as a favorite. I only went to school looking for a fight, not to have fun playing, learning, or being a supportive teammate. Ask another child about middle school and they might smile, remembering the good days. Ask me about middle school and I frown, remembering the fights. That's how my fury controlled me as a young girl. I was pinned in, boxed on all sides by a wrath that demanded my obedience. The journey of my life has been dedicated to breaking out of this fortress, freeing myself from the hopelessness of seeing red all the time. And I know this for sure – if I can crawl out of the misery of my heart burning up in a state of constant outrage, you can do it too.

73

After almost 20 years of watching the anger destroy so many lives, the realization came to me that I was stuck on anger all my early years and I made things worse for myself. I never had the joy of a high school experience, the excitement of the first day of a new year of learning. I never went to the Prom. I regret that to this day. My indignation at everything made me a ball of irritation walking down the hallway on the rare days when I actually entered the school building. There was no one to help me because I would never let anyone enter my space without paying a price – without being cursed out or attacked. I didn't know any better, but looking back, I didn't know why. I remember being lonely and feeling isolated; I was bitter and enraged that someone or something had made me so anti-social and I didn't even know what or who it was that made me that way. There was no help for me. But this book is help for you. I hope it helps you find your problem. I hope you see yourself in my struggles. And I hope you see yourself in the struggles of some of the young people I've mentioned.

As I got older, I realized I was angry at my parents for their fights on Saturday nights. I hated their divorce. I didn't understand that parents have troubles between themselves and it didn't mean that they didn't love me or that I was responsible for the troubles they had. I grabbed onto the fact of their fighting and took it down the road to anger. Nothing could stop me at that point because I thought I was justified to feel the way I did. Anger creates its own justification, like a marker in the ground, as though it is saying, "This is my territory and nothing can change it." I got stuck. As a child, there was no therapist to unravel my feelings and help me put them in perspective. Many years later, I came to realize I couldn't blame my anger on my parents, who worked really hard and protected me as well as they could. The problem was anger itself. When I gave anger the opening to enter my heart and build its fortress there, I cut off every chance there was to understand why I had become so enraged. My brothers and sisters lived through the same circumstances and their reactions were different than mine. Like a child who has a need for drugs built into his or her genes, I must have had the seeds of anger in my soul, somewhere a 10 year old couldn't know anything about, just waiting to be fertilized by a set of traumatic events. It has been a long journey to reach this understanding and now I can reveal the secret that brings the healing: it is forgiveness. The more I learned to forgive my parents, the more my anger dissolved. The more I learned to forgive myself, the more I could allow myself to be loved by others. The more I learned to forgive, the less I had to forgive. My anger dissolved like ice melting in the sun. Forgiveness is the antidote for anger.

Forgiveness is also the first step for breaking the cycle of anger that moves from generation to generation. It is the cycle of pain that gets passed on from mother to child. The child grows up, has a baby and treats her child the same way. When you learn to forgive the ones who hurt you, a dam breaks and the anger flows out of your heart like water running down a hill. Now *you're* in control. You can control the impulse so you don't do the same hurtful things to those around you or to your own children.

If you've known this kind of anger, the kind that jumps up out of nowhere, over nothing, and stays until the day is a wreck, remember you can break the cycle by embracing your children, showering them with hugs and kisses. Nothing says to a child, "You don't have to be angry," like a big hug from mom or a kiss on the forehead from dad. When you have children, talk to them in a way that shows they are important, significant individuals worthy of conversation and patience and understanding. When there's trouble with the spouse or the boyfriend or girlfriend, talk to the children so they know everything is okay at home.

There may be fights and arguments in the house, no place is perfect, but when the dust settles, you have to make the children feel safe by communicating that everything is fine, there's no need to worry, there's no need for the child to be angry and mad just because the grown-ups got irritated at each other. Find ways to help the child let out his or her pent-up feelings, without judgment or punishment or criticism. If there's a divorce, no matter the pain involved, talk about it with the children so they don't blame themselves for the separation. This keeps them from getting stuck in a cycle of anger, bad behavior, more anger and escalating resentment about all the minor things that become irritants in their everyday lives. Remember, when there's a fight in your house on Saturday night, there may be a fight on the way to school on Monday morning, a teacher may get a cursed out on Tuesday, or a younger sister may get her tooth punched out on Wednesday. When you have children, talk to them when trouble comes around. Let the air out, like you would a tire that has been over inflated. Anger can't compete with reason. It dies when mom or dad says to a child, "Tell me how that made you feel?" Anger melts, like snow in the sun, when you hug your child and say, "Mommy made a mistake and I will try to never do that again."

When I was stuck on anger, I made things worse for myself. I didn't know the power of forgiveness. I didn't know how to forgive my parents. I didn't know how to forgive the girls who referred to me as "a white girl." I didn't know how to forgive the white people who I thought looked down at me and judged me in a negative way. I was stuck in the moment when my co-workers called me "nigger lover" during my painting career as a young adult. I couldn't get over the injustice and meanness of them using that term. Even though I had information that suggested the opposite, my dogged anger locked me into the belief that all white people were the same, all of them thinking I was "a nigger lover." I carried this bitterness for years and looked for every opportunity to feed it more proof. Some of the proof was manufactured and rehearsed in my own mind.

For example, I thought my vocabulary didn't meet white people's standards, because I was raised in the inner city and had dropped out of high school. That's enough to make you mad, although it was never true.

Over many years of watching others struggle with anger, building great walls to keep their anger in and all positive thoughts out, I came to realize the wrath toward white people was all in my imagination. Yes, some dumb co-workers called me "a nigger lover," but they were idiots, trapped in their own ignorance, searching for some stupid way to make themselves feel important by trashing others. The use of the term "nigger lover" said more about them than it did about me. To take that filthy comment and use it as a measure to judge all white people is a prime example of what anger did to spoil my outlook. My anger would have me believe, "All white people talk and feel that way!" I get stuck there. Every time I saw a white person, I would hear the phrase, "a nigger lover," coming out of their mouths, even if they were really smiling, saying, "Hello, how are you; I hope you have a nice day." The anger says, "Don't trust what you hear; that's the cover-up. Deep down, he or she thinks you're a nigger lover!" You can't get away from the resentment because you're stuck in it. You can't accept the kind hand reaching out to you because your prejudice prejudges the gesture with a term like "nigger lover" that makes your blood boil with hatred. I had to come to the realization that it was me who had taken a bad experience and turned it into a furious determination to dislike a whole race of people I didn't even know. Anger works in undercover ways. It tricked me into being stuck by taking the ugly attitude of a few and applying it to everyone. How convenient and easy that was. Anger likes it that way. "Don't give anyone a chance to be kind and supportive and loving," anger says. Then you didn't have to build relationships based on trust and consistency. Anger kills trust in the beginning. Consistency has no chance. I began to see that, in giving into the anger, I was my own worst enemy. I was sabotaging myself and my future.

The more I learned and interacted with all kinds of people, the more I realized that no one was better than me or worse than me simply because of the color of his or her skin, or the way he or she dressed, or the manner in which he or she spoke. These were powerful realizations that turned my anger upside down.

I discovered traits that I needed to work on if I was going to squeeze the rage out of my heart. Think about these traits listed below and ask yourself, "Is that me?"

1) Closing off, no one allowed in

2) Trusting no one
3) Harboring negative opinions, quick to judge
4) Irritating, angry at small things
5) Complaining all the time
6) Isolating myself
7) Shunning positive relationships.
8) Fighting, quick to argue
9) Thinking someone is out to get me
10) Abandoning love
11) Blaming others
12) Taking no responsibility
13) Avoiding every chance to learn

Each one of these conditions links with the other. They can weight down a little heart and turn a normally happy child into a bad-tempered, bitter ball of meanness almost overnight. But not just a child. These same traits can be signs that any of us are stuck on anger, battling demons of pain that hide behind high walls, influencing our reactions to spouses, family members and friends. The pain spoke to anger and said, "You be my protector, you be my defense, so I don't have to remember and no one can make me talk about what happened that hurt me so much." Anger steps up and says, "I'm your man!" But we don't have to sit back and let anger rule. We can fight back. I didn't have any help with these things when I was young, but my journey prepared me to help others who were faced with the same kinds of trauma.

During my professional years as a group home provider, I witnessed firsthand the hurt and pain young girls carried in their hearts. Many blamed the foster care system for not allowing them to visit their family members on a regular basis or be placed back home. For example, one girl who was in my care said, "As soon as I was admitted into the foster care system I became angry. I didn't care. The court system promised me and my sister that we would go home soon and soon never came around. I was promised that I would go home with my mother. That never happened. My anger would continue to build because I was lied too. I did not trust the foster care system." The anger she felt ruined everything positive every day.

Most of the girls believed that there was no hope for them to go home because there was no stable home environment to return to. Some of the girls knew in their hearts and minds that they better make the best of their current situations.

Nearly all of the girls in my care were stuck on anger and confused about their lives. School was not important to most of them. One girl with whom I worked said, "I struggled all the time. I felt like I was labeled because I had a special education plan and I lived in a group home. I struggled with my friends and teachers because I felt like I was being judged by everyone. I was angry all the time and dared someone to say something to me."

The anger that engulfed their lives occupied all of their attention. It was survival! I often imagined myself in their situations, removed from my mother and family members due to no fault of my own, living away from home, strangers telling me when to eat, sleep, and shower. Yes! As a teenager, I would have been hurt too – angry and ready to explode.

My job was to love the girls, to give them unconditional feelings of support and understanding. Many of the girls expressed disappointment in their mothers' life choices. Most didn't know their fathers. I remembered my own experiences that had me stuck on anger. I had to draw back on my own healing, where I came to the realization that blaming my parents and others got me nowhere. I started taking responsibility for my own actions. I wanted to help these girl do the same.

When the girls shared their feelings regarding the anger they held toward their mothers who hurt them, I immediately tried to bring balance to the discussion. I wanted the girls to learn their mothers' stories. "Believe me," I said, "Your mother feels guilty, ashamed and sorry for what she did when you were young. It couldn't have turned out worse – she used drugs, lost her baby and can't even get permission to spend two hours with you without somebody else being in the room. Now that's punishment." The mothers made bad choices and, as a consequence, their kids were gone, taken from their home because the state deemed their homes unsafe places for children.

One parent with whom I worked was a recovering addict who tried hard to get her kids back from the foster care system. I felt her remorse. "My baby don't trust me," she said, adding, "I can't do nothing to fix this." She said, "My big mistake was falling in love when I was younger, only to find out that he wasn't worth nothing, a drug dealer all the way." Before she knew it, she had two children. By that time, she was using and abusing drugs, neglecting her children and child protective services stepped in and took her kids from the home.

It took ten years, but eventually she enrolled in a long-term drug treatment program. That's when I met her, ten years after her children had been in foster care, ten years after her children had been bounced from family to family, group home to group home. For her kids, the anger built up like scar tissue, bitter hard resentment colored their personalities, made them stuck in the same angry place. "It's taken all this time," the mother said, "for me to realize how bad a mother I've been to my kids." It was like watching someone on a sky-high tightrope, as she worked hard to stay clean, struggling and praying for a positive relationship with the child who was in my care. Ten years is a long time, and, for the child, the accumulated disappointment and anger wouldn't give in easily.

And then the parent relapsed. It was heartbreaking. Back again to drugs and the streets. "I am so sorry, Sylvia," she said in a late night call from a phone booth, sounding like tears were running down her face. "I ain't worth nothing and my baby is dying because of me." "You have to keep trying," I told her, "you have to get back to rehab and prove that your daughter is more important to you than drugs."

To the daughter, my message was, "Forgive you mother, because she's sick. She trying, but she's limited. She loves you, yet she doesn't know how to show it. Give her a chance, because she didn't mean to hurt you." We talked and talked. My job with the girls was to deescalate the negative feelings toward their mothers. This process took months, even years. "It's not easy to stop using drugs," I told the daughter, "to become productive and take responsibility to get a home, pay rent, keep it clean and put food on the table. The addiction is embedded in your mother. You have to understand this and let go of the negative anger toward her." A refusal to let the anger go backfires on the one who was hurt in the first place. "But, listen, you can't be angry at your mother forever," I said, "it only makes you stuck on anger and being stuck will destroy your life."

After 20 years, I realized these girls needed mothers, fathers and family members to feel connected to the world, no matter what the circumstance may have been. Even the ones who had been treated the worst still longed for their parents. I had two sisters whose mother and father were on death row for murder. One girl was a cutter, a self-mutilator; the other couldn't stay put long enough to establish any relationships. And, still, they wanted their parents. While reunification wasn't going to work for these two young girls, it was essential to make the effort for others. Some social workers said, "There are drugs and gangs in that neighborhood." I said, "Drugs, alcohol, and gangs are everywhere in our communities, including in the schools." For me, it was a choice between keeping them away from their parents or serving them up on a platter for anger. I had seen and lived the ravages of anger. I thought getting them back with their families, even if the families were imperfect, was the best way to help them heal.

Sometimes the best social workers, and there were many, listened and would let me try to bring daughters and mothers together. Even when it happened, the anger didn't want to easily give up and walk away. The anger started working other angles. Anger stood up and whispered lies to my girls, "Okay, you were mad when you couldn't be with your mom, now, no matter how hard your mother tries, you have to hold on to being enraged at your mom, make sure you punish her for losing you to the system in the first place!" Anger tried to destroy trust before trust had a chance. With anger whispering in her ear, it was easy for the girls to replay the same question over and over – "Is my mother going to meet a guy and runoff and start using drugs again?"

And the mother was at a loss. She had never been a mother. She had never put her feelings in a secondary position in relation to her daughter's feelings. She had never carried on discussions about how her daughter felt. Her daughter comes to the reunion with all these brand new hopes, thinking, "Mom is going to love me and talk to me and hold me when I cry." But that might not be her mom. Mom might be cold and distant, because she doesn't know what to do or what to say. Her mom is not capable of dealing with the layers of pain and hurt that have accumulated in her child. They are stacked as high as a mountain. So the mother she expects, the one she dreams about and hopes for, may not be the mother she gets. I told the child, "Forgive her." I told the mom, "Be patient, talk to her, listen to her, admit that you did things wrong but now you want to do things right." Her daughter was stuck in anger and resentment and we had to help her learn to let the past go.

Not only did I have to deal with the girls stuck on anger and mothers struggling to change, I had to deal with some less than enlightened social workers who refused to allow family visits. I saw this differently. No matter what the mother had done, the young girl in foster care wanted nothing more than to be with her mother. It's a need like air and water. The mother might be a drug addict, a prostitute or mentally challenged, but being taken away leaves a traumatic scar that feeds the anger of foster girls. It makes them stuck, braced by anger on all sides, unable to build relationships, unable to perform in school, unable to allow a caring teacher to show them the way, unable to find any peace in their lives. "She can't go back into that drug infested place," the social worker said, adding, "I am not going to take the responsibility if something should go wrong, so the answer is NO." I argued, "Her mom is trying to get off drugs, she going to rehab, she's got a place to stay and she is trying so hard to make up for her mistakes. We have a choice between a bad environment with her mom or a child being penned in anger, sabotaging every good opportunity in her life. Let her see her mother in short supervised visits first. The more we keep her from her mother, the more she wants to be with her mother. We're breeding the anger by saying NO."

CHAPTER 7

TURNING POINTS IN MY LIFE

There were several turning points in my life that assisted and prepared me to confront and conquer my anger. One turning point was when I applied for a non-profit status and was approved in April, 1994. One year later, I was granted a license to open a group home by the State of California's Community Care Licensing Division. My life changed the day I began caring for traumatized girls who were maltreated and angry at their parents or others who hurt them.

A second turning point in my life took place when I was accepted in a doctorate program in 2010. One of the requirements in the program was to form a team of three committee members with doctorate degrees who could mentor me through the program. It took me one year to find a Chair and two years to find two committee members. In the meantime, I was in class doing my course work.

My studies focused the secondary school experience of ex-foster care Hispanic and African American women 19-26 who lived in my group homes. I wanted to find out how they perceived their experiences in high school while they lived in group homes during their teenage years. I witnessed firsthand the struggles many of the girls had in high school trying to build positive relationships with their peers, teachers, and parents. I saw their anger in living color, an anger that prevented them from having success in high school or building positive relationships.

My studies confirmed what I already knew. Some people who store anger and refuse to uncover its sources turn to bad behaviors and habits that bring ruin to their lives, such as violence, drugs, meaningless sex, and alcohol abuse. Others blame people for the destructive behaviors that are the outcomes of their anger. Blaming others is a good way to avoid the difficult process of identifying the ones who hurt you, how they hurt you and what you can do about overcoming the pain. Anger likes having a shadowy past, a situation where its' roots are hidden and never confronted. Healing begins with the courage to ask honest questions. Do you think you have anger issues hidden in your soul? Do you have hurt and pain that won't go away? Is a general negative view of life lurking behind the face you put on everyday? Ask yourselves these questions:

1. Are you unhappy in your current situation? And if so, why?
2. Are you unhappy with your attitudes and behaviors? And if so, why?
3. Are you unhappy with yourself? If so, why?
4. Are you holding on to past pain and hurt? And if so, why?
5. Are you ready to uncover your anger? If not, why not?
6. Are you ready to forgive the ones who hurt you? If not, why not?
7. Do you feel you are trapped in anger? If so, why?

8. Do you feel your life is out of control? And if so, why?

In my studies, I read several articles by Dr. Robert Enright, a scholar at the University of Wisconsin. Dr. Enright's theory focused on anger and the importance of learning to forgive the wrongdoers. Over the past four decades, he has written several books and over a hundred scholarly articles on anger and forgiveness. Dr. Enright said anger destroys people mentally if they allow the anger to control them. Dr. Enright's method on forgiveness was exciting to me. After purchasing many of his books and reading his materials for two years, I realized, in my own way, I was already practicing his approach in my group homes with the girls.

One day I wrote Dr. Enright a letter, asking if he would consider mentoring me through my educational journey by becoming a member of my committee. That was November, 2013. A few weeks had passed and I didn't hear from him, so I sent him an email follow-up.

Shortly after Thanksgiving, at six o'clock in the morning, I received an email from Dr. Enright, saying he would be honored to be part of my committee. This was another major turning point in my life. A world renowned scholar on the act and practice of forgiveness said, "Yes, I will work with you!" At first, I couldn't believe it. I pinched myself, reading the email three more times. With tears in my eyes, I jumped up, ran to my bedroom to tell my husband. It seemed like I cried that entire week, sharing the good news with everyone. I was overwhelmed with enthusiasm for this opportunity to learn.

Dr. Enright's theory on forgiveness had been around for many decades. His approach is excellent for individuals who want to uncover their anger and work on forgiving the wrongdoers. Dr. Enright said people can be stuck in anger and layers of anger will build, creating all sorts of mental health problems. The sources of the anger have to be addressed. I truly believed in his theory because my life proved he was right.

Dr. Enright's Forgiveness Education is a powerful tool that was perfectly suited for me in my effort to help the girls in the group home. Through this approach, many of the girls were eventually set free from the bondage of the anger and bitterness that had ruled their lives for years. Forgiveness Education is a step toward healing, said Dr. Enright.

CHAPTER 8

WORKING ON FORGIVENESS

Forgiveness Education centers on four phases and offers a list of questions to be asked of angry individuals who want to learn to forgive the people who hurt them. The four phases of Forgiveness Education include:

Phase 1 … Uncovering anger
Phase 2 … Deciding to forgive
Phase 3 … Working on forgiveness
Phase 4 … Releasing the pain and anger

Following Dr. Enright's forgiveness approach, I developed questions that helped my girls navigate the process in each phase.

Phase 1 -- Uncovering Anger

a) Who are you angry with?
b) Are you ready to work on your anger problems?

When I conducted group sessions with my young ladies in foster care, we sat around a large living room that had a big classroom size white board on the wall. Each girl had a clipboard with blank paper to write on. I used a teacher-led approach. In the first question, I asked these youngsters who were they angry with? Almost all of them said, "My mother!" I asked them to list reasons why they were angry with their mothers. We read the reasons out loud.

One teenager said, with tears rolling down her face, "I don't understand why my mother is using drugs when she knows what it does to her. And what it does to me and my brothers and sisters. I will never be able to go home."

Another said, "My mother likes living on the streets and drinking with her friends. She never thinks about me or my brothers."

And yet another shared her feelings, saying, "If my mother could find herself a full-time job, she can get a house and me and my siblings can go back home to live together."

This is the uncovering phase – saying things out loud that before were just innermost thoughts.

While other teenagers know their parents, see them every day, my girls worried about the wellbeing of the mothers they never saw. They dealt with the realization that their relationships, or lack of relationships, with their mothers were different than other kids. It made them feel abnormal. They felt it was unfair. Very few had weekend visits with their mothers. Very few visited other family members. Most of these girls didn't have approval from their county social workers to see their mothers, primarily because the social workers feared the unsafe surroundings in which the mothers lived.

"I hate not knowing where my mother is or who she is with," one said. "Why do I have to go through this?"

It was a question that had no decent, acceptable answer. This was a constant irritation, like fingernails persistently scraping across a blackboard. The question created one endless bad mood. For my girls, with this bleeding sore in their hearts, it became difficult to concentrate on education when everything served up resentment, constantly reminding them that they were living in a different world than other young people their ages.

"I'm so lonely, I don't fit anywhere, I don't have a chance," one child said out loud as she began to uncover the roots of her anger.

In the uncovering phase, things come out, things that had been buried, that no one else had ever heard.

"I worry about my brothers and sisters. Will I ever see them again; will we ever be able to go back home? Will I be able to visit them or any of my family?"

They didn't expect their mothers to suddenly change. Still, some held out the hope that one day they could go back home and be with their families. Hope is a funny thing. The existence of it can be a positive motivator. But the fact that one has to "hope" for something as basic as a relationship with one's mother creates resentment and anger. I told my girls, "Holding on to past anger and resentment toward your mothers will destroy every new chance you have to be happy, to make a friend or to learn in school. It's not healthy." We had to be honest. But I know from experience that anger hates honesty. When I was young, anything that looked or sounded like an honest criticism was enough to make me unleash a furious attack. I walked around literally daring someone to tell me the truth. When the actor in the movie, *"A Few Good Men,"* said, "You can't handle the truth," he could have been speaking to the anger in us. On the one hand, nearly all my young ladies blamed their anger on their mothers; on the other hand, none of them were unwilling to even entertain, much less acknowledge, that they were responsible for the hurt their anger inflected on others. This was my time to teach: "You can't change your mothers' choices' and the damage those choices did to you. You can't change that. But you don't have to let the pain of those choices ruin the rest of your lives and make the people around you miserable. Your mother made the choices that got you here; now you have a chance to make better choices and allowing anger to dominate your behavior can't be one of them. The honest truth is that you're in control now."

This was our chance to uncover the anger and start the forgiving process. I couldn't let them leave my care with anger stored up, burning them up inside, always ready to scorch any generous hand that reached out to help. I knew unaddressed anger would dribble out in every area of their lives. That anger breeds bitterness and self-destruction. Uncovering the source of the anger is the first step, a hard step, but a necessary step.

Although a therapist worked in the group home, many of the girls refused to speak to her as a way of reaching out for help. One girl said, "The way I cope with my feelings is by cutting/hurting myself. I never expressed my feelings to a therapist. I would only talk to her about my relationships with my peers or other people. I always refused to speak to a therapist. I didn't want to tell her my feelings."

This is how the anger builds, when they refuse to talk about it, refuse to identify where it comes from. I could see that the anger was being stored within and that eventually it would explode. It was sad to see them refuse the help of a therapist. I knew that if they wouldn't uncover the anger with a therapist, it had to be done in group sessions. Either way, the past hurt and pain had to be exposed.

Indignant about the mistakes of her mother, one girl said, "When I do visit my mother, she goes into the bedroom with her boyfriend and leaves me in the living room, but I don't care because at least I have a chance to see her."

Another girl said, "I hate when my mom puts her boyfriends before me."

Imagine the feeling: the person who is supposed to take care of you, guide you and protect you still puts a boyfriend above you, even after you've been taken away from her by the state. That's a powerful negative image, a breeding ground for rage.

What was important during these weekly group sessions was to have the girls share their deep-rooted feelings about their mothers. I listened as they expressed their past hurt and pain. In the uncovering process, revelations are a combination of fear and relief. The expressions on their faces showed rage and resentment as they described the circumstances surrounding their mothers, some on drugs, some living on the streets, some selling their bodies just to get by, some in drug treatment programs, and some in prison. I also heard the love they had for their mothers, I could feel it. Looking back on my life, I realized I loved my mother regardless of what happened to me. I will always love my mother. As the young ladies uncovered their anger, I wanted them to have compassion for their mothers' problems, whatever they may be experiencing. It was important to learn from their mothers' mistakes and not repeat the same things. "Uncover this anger," I told our group, "The anger you are carrying in your hearts and minds toward your mothers has to be let go. It's the only way you can heal from the impact of all the negative experiences that produced the anger controlling your destructive behaviors."

One daughter said, "I hate my mother. She lies to me all the time. She always says she will get herself in a drug treatment program. But she never does."

I always tried hard to convince her and the others that, "You shouldn't be so hard on your mother. Your attitude will make healing impossible. Whenever you do spend time with your mother, you have to enjoy every minute." I had seen so many young women get an opportunity to be with their mothers and squander it away. They allowed the anger to spoil the moment they had been wishing for. The person they wanted most to be close to them was pushed away by accusations and meanness. It was the opposite of what the girls really wanted. They begged to be allowed to see their mothers but, when they got the chance, the rage inside took over and "I hate you" came charging out. Questions, laced with accusations, came next: "Why did you allow this to happen to me?" "Why are you such a bad mother?" "Did you even care about me at all?" The meeting they had hoped for and dreamt about actually dug the hole of anger even deeper. When they had the chance to meet with their mothers, anger ruined the opportunity, just like it ruined all other relationships with peers and teachers and counselors. This was not uncovering anger, it was being the victim of it.

Anger never wants to be analyzed and evaluated. It prefers to lurk in the shadows and jump out in an explosion that no one really understands. In the process of forgiveness, uncovering anger means that we bring it into the light. When this happens, anger can no longer hide in the darkness and jump out whenever it wants to, making us ruin a good day, or a new friendship, or a reunion with our moms. Uncovering anger means putting a spotlight on it. A spotlight makes anger scatter for cover, like roaches.

To bring it all out in the light, I started by asking all the girls to write their feelings on paper, starting with who they're angry with and are they ready to uncover that anger?

We had to get those feelings out, to expose the anger in public, in front of me and their peers. Remember, anger likes to be confined inside, out of sight. It hides in the bushes, underneath the carpet, behind the curtain, any place where it can't be seen or observed.

One in the group admitted, "I am so mad all the time. I walk around just waiting for someone to say something to me, to mess with me in any way, so I can attack and get in trouble. I don't feel anything when I strike out at somebody. I let the urge eat me up. I get wasted almost, like I'm being used by a force outside me. When it's over, I just go to sleep, maybe all day."

Admitting those things, saying them out loud, with others listening, in public, meant she was ready to acknowledge the pain of the past and begin to let it go. I said, "I am proud that you recognize the reality of the circumstances that created your anger. This is one step toward the healing process."

The uncovering phase is a challenge because you have to do something new and strange – open up! Thoughts and feelings that have never been shared get exposed. It's scary. Anger holds on to these thoughts and feelings like a stingy man clings to money. The moment you open up to identifying where the pain comes from, anger starts losing its grip. If there is no desire to forgive, the angry person has to hold the pain and hurt inside to fuel the fire of resentment and bitterness. For the one who wants to forgive, opening up creates a sense of relief. By talking and writing about it, anger loses its domination. It is a relief to see that anger does not have to be the dominant powerful unrelenting second personality that makes you the ugliest person on the block, in school or at home. When you open up, it's a relief because you no longer have to deny the existence of anger. No more excuses for why you were mean and vicious to a teacher. No more justifications for bruising a classmate's face. No more twisted efforts to make anger right and everybody else wrong. Anger is not a friend. It's an enemy. In the openness of the uncovering phase, the truth comes out. Anger is unwrapped and just about finished

One girl said, "When I was placed in a foster home, I was not mad at first, but after a week or so, I became angry because

I was away from my family. My mom used to hit me hard. That was why I ended up in the system. But I started missing my family. I became angry and wanted to go back home. I felt like I was not a bad person. I was just frustrated about my home situation."

There is a shame that comes with explosive anger. You can't explain why you cursed out the teacher who tried to help you. You can't explain why you frowned at the classmate who simply said, "Good morning." There's no way to explain how mean and ugly you were to the clerk at the store. There is a shame that comes with behaving in ways that are hurtful and wicked. Before it gets exposed, anger sits on one side, encouraging you to be disagreeable and nasty to everyone. The better part of you sits on the other side, saying, "Why did you do that? Why are you so mean? That teacher was trying to help you! That girl at school was just saying, hello."

When you open up and the light shines in, anger gets weak. It loses its toxic power to make you do atrocious things to others. The better side starts living. And there is no more reason to be ashamed.

Start by uncovering the source of your pain and suffering. Talk about it with teachers, counselors, and friends, journal about it, don't be afraid to open up and let the truth come out.

Phase 2 -- Deciding to Forgive.

a) Can you identify the ones who hurt you?
b) Are you ready to forgive them?

c)   Are you ready to forgive yourself?

Who did this to you? Was it your mother who abandoned you, neglected you, left you uncared for in dangerous situations? Were you mistreated? Were you disciplined harshly, whipped with a belt or a switch? Were you homeless, living underneath a bridge? Who did this? Who hurt you? I wanted each girl to say the names of those who caused her hurt and pain. This is no time to be timid. There is no room to protect someone. Pain in young hearts is an odd thing, especially when it comes from mothers. A rationalization comes into play – a child might think: I hate what happened to me but I don't want to tell anybody how I really feel because it may make my mom feel badly. Anger loves this type of conflict. It exploits the fear of telling the truth. But I told my girls, "No one is off limits here. And we're not sugar-coating the truth. It might be hard to say that your mom was a bad parent. Remember, we're not here to hurt your mom. We're here to save your life!"

This worked. The truth started coming out and the room became electric. As one spoke, another nodded. The expression of truth was contagious. One of the younger teenage girls said, "It was my mother who hurt me. She left me home with my brothers and sister so she could go be with her boyfriend and use drugs." Another said, "My mother left me with my grandma to raise me because she wanted to go use drugs and hang-out with her friends."

The identification question is important. It brings clarity and focus to the source of your pain. Anger hates that. Anger operates best when the feeling of resentment comes from an unknown, but powerful, place. Then anger can jump out at anyone at any time, like a time bomb that has someone else's finger on the trigger. Bring a little clarity to the picture and anger loses its cover and justification. In our group sessions, I literally saw anger leaving the hearts of the girls, stomping out of the room like a spoiled child no longer the center of attention, no longer getting it's way. As they let the pain go by identifying those who hurt them, their eyes softened, voices changed, smiles replaced hard faces, laughter erupted, and we felt like we were a real team with everybody pulling in the same direction, trying to win the game against anger.

Answering the second question, "are you ready to forgive," all of them were willing to make the decision to forgive the ones who hurt them, specifically, their mothers.

"I am ready to forgive my mother," one girl said. "I really feel sorry for my mother," another said, "because she seems confused about what she wants out of her life and I am seeing I cannot help her." I said, "You are right, she is the adult and you have to learn to help yourself and love and forgive your mother."

When I asked the girls if they were ready to forgive their mothers, I knew that this was not an easy step. Saying out loud that you want to forgive is like a promissory note for barrowed money – eventually you have to honor it. There is something special about making a commitment to forgive another person who has done you wrong. It's scary. Saying you will forgive makes you vulnerable. So I said, "Make sure you think about this step and don't take it lightly. It's a road you're deciding to take. It won't be easy, but, in the end, you will have a chance to find joy and peace in spite of the pain you've experienced in your life. Are you ready?"

"Yes, I will make an effort," said one girl. "It may be hard for me to forgive my mother because all she does is lie to me and it makes me hate her," a second young lady said. "I'll try, but, still, I don't think she'll ever change," another mentioned with muffled hope. Eventually they all said they were willing to try.

It took some time but, in the end, they understood that the choice wasn't about saving their mothers' lives but saving their own. It helped when I said, "Forgiveness is a gift you give yourself. It's selfish, like buying a Christmas present for yourself and putting it under the tree with your mother's name on it. It keeps on giving. Your mother gets the benefit of being forgiven for all her mistakes. You get in touch with human feelings you have never felt before. Kindness. Generosity. Love. Joy. Happiness. And you're the one with the smile on your face, you're the one in control."

Saying, "Yes, I forgive," puts anger in retreat mode. It's like pushing the mute button on anger's anti-social voice. Anger can't tell you to curse out your teachers for trying to help you with your school lessons. You can't hear anger when it wants you to fight a classmate over nothing. Anger is in trouble now. The voice of ugliness and evil and meanness is on mute. Saying, "Yes, I forgive," is a death sentence for anger.

Taking a stroll down memory lane, I told them my story. I saw my parents fighting and I internalized what I saw in a way that made me a ball of anger. I cursed. I fought. I looked for reasons to be mean. When I was young, I had no idea where all this hostility came from. I was mean to my family. For me, anger was like a bodyguard that bullied others, took offense at every glance, and spoiled relationships before they could even grow. Later, opening the group home and working with girls who were angry like me, I realized it was me, not my parents. I had to forgive them, not because they did anything wrong, but because my anger forced me to blame them. I had to decide to forgive. When I did that, I came to the conclusion that it wasn't them at all. I was in control. I didn't have to give into the anger in the way that I did. Any blame I put on my mother and father was wrong. Forgiveness allowed me to see that and it has made my life so much better. It is draining to hate and curse and fight and plant misery everywhere you go. It's like living in the gutter. Contrast that to feeling happy, joyful, friendly, loving and peaceful all the time just by saying, "Yes, I forgive."

Finally, I asked, probably the most important question, "Are you ready to forgive yourself?" Sounds simple, but it's not. Anger has controlled their lives. Anger is ugly. Anger makes us do vicious things to innocent people. My girls had cursed out teachers, picked fights with peers, screamed at their mothers, and called family members horrible names. They had cut on themselves and turned their pain into an indictment of themselves, as though they were hurt in life because they deserved to be hurt. It's a self-fulfilling prophecy of anger. My anger makes me hates others. Consequently, I hate myself. I said, "Only the decision to forgive yourself can reverse the self-hatred that anger breeds."

First, I asked them to give up the shame. We had identified

the source of the pain and hurt. We had made a decision to forgive those who hurt us. Now we can let go of the pain that creates the anger. And we can forgive ourselves for whatever we did in those angry moments when resentment and bitterness ruled our lives. There is nothing to cover up anymore. The pain has been openly acknowledged. I encouraged the girls to forgive themselves for all they had done to cover up their hurt and pain with anger. No more feelings of guilt and shame for their responses to what had happened to them in their lives.

Second, I asked them if they thought they deserved forgiveness. So many of these foster girls blamed themselves for their conditions. One young girl in my care had been placed in the foster care system when she was three years old. Her mother was in and out of drug treatment programs and prison. Her grandmother adopted her to prevent her from staying in the foster system. This child loved her grandma and enjoyed the one-on-one attention she received. At nine, she came home from school and found her grandmother dead, lying in the bathtub, her clothes on, no water in the tub. This traumatized this young lady for years. She *blamed* herself. Had she come home earlier, she told herself, she could have saved her grandmother. It wasn't her fault. My job was to teach her that she had to be kind to herself and let that burden go.

It wasn't their fault their mothers used drugs. They didn't do anything to deserve being left alone for days at a time. Uncovering the truth helps make this clear. They had no control over any of this. When they put it in perspective, identifying the true source of their agony, then they had the basis to forgive themselves. All of a sudden, a spotlight sparkled on their good qualities. They opened up to the teacher who wanted to help them learn in school. They showed kindness to a friend. Something inside allowed them to feel generosity and a giving spirit. I said, "You have to love yourself for who you are and be proud of who you are. We're not looking back, we're looking at their future."

One young girl said, "I never understood what it meant to forgive myself for my mistakes. I just always thought there was something wrong with me." I said, "In order for you to move forward in life, you must forgive yourself first. You can't keep pounding yourself into the dirt over the ugly things you've done. This is a new day, a fresh start."

Forgiveness is a repair shop that fixes all the mental wounds and scars of the past. Forgiveness allows the cuts, breaks, and bruises to start healing. Like a broken arm or leg, the healing may not happen overnight but I said, "Girls, you all have the power within you to forgive yourselves so that you can move forward to forgive whoever hurt you."

It's a good way forward. Step 1, we admit where the pain and hurt comes from. Step 2, we decide to forgive those who hurt us. Step 3, we decide to forgive ourselves. Now it's time to get down to work.

Phase 3 -- Working on Forgiveness

> a) Are you ready to work on acceptance?
> b) Are you ready to work on compassion?

Forgiveness is a process that takes practice. The first thing I asked my girls to do was find the love in their hearts.

Tell me, I said, what you love about your mothers. I asked them to list the things they treasured. I wanted them to write about enjoyable memories, to remember and focus on the good times, setting the negative feelings aside. I got goose bumps the moment they caught on. It was beautiful and uplifting to hear the stories.

One girl said, "I remember me and my mother going shopping for clothes and we tried on the same types of clothes. It was so much fun." Another girl said, "I remember helping my mother cook for Thanksgiving. We picked up the turkey and we played with it while we were seasoning it." There was one girl who said, "I like just spending time with my mother watching movies and eating popcorn with my brothers and little sisters."

One of the girls started crying when she described her home life during Christmas time. She said, "My mom would wake us up at midnight and make hot chocolate at let me and my brothers and sister open up our gifts." When she shared her story, she cried. The other girls started crying. And I cried.

Forgiving the ones who hurt you, or yourself for that matter, can't be done if you remember all the bad things that happened. I wanted them to remember the good things because I know anger can't survive in a positive atmosphere. How can you be angry when you're laughing about seasoning a turkey together on Thanksgiving? You can't be angry when you're smiling about the movie you saw with your family! Or how much fun you had at Christmas time! Each girl had memories of special times with their mothers and each one smiled when they expressed the story. This told me that forgiveness was working because they wanted it to work.

Acceptance was so important at this stage. They had to accept their mothers in order to forgive them, in order to love them. I always remember the theologian's advice, "God grant me the serenity to accept the things I cannot change, the courage to change the things I can, and the wisdom to know the difference." I wanted them to accept the acknowledgment of the circumstances that hurt them. They had to recognize their mothers' mistakes. There is no way to change what happened. Accept it, let the pain and hurt go. In the case of my girls, acceptance meant loving their mothers even if their mothers continued to do unacceptable things.

Accepting that "my mother is a dope head and she'll always be a dope head," as one girl put it, is a tough thing to face. Embracing the notion that "my mom likes living under the bridges because she always ends up there, no matter how much support she gets" is difficult to say, much less believe as the truth. I said, "Working on forgiveness involves being honest enough to accept your mom right where she is. If you don't accept her, you won't be able to find the strength to forgive her."

Each girl had to accept themselves as well. Yes, they were abused. Yes, they are in foster care. And, yes, they may never get to live at home with their mothers before getting out of high school. In response to all that, they had acted out in terrible ways. All hard realities. I said, "Accept all that and move on." Forgiveness doesn't sugar coat the reality. If you have to sugar coat the circumstances, you're leaving behind pieces of the disease of anger. The pieces will come back to get you later. To forgive yourself, you've got to remember exactly how you acted when you got suspended at school – when your teacher said, "Where's your homework?" and you threw your papers at her and said, "Bitch, you're not my mother!" It was ugly and unnecessary. Forgiveness can handle a reality that is not so pretty. Each girl had to look honestly at what they had done and say, "I forgive." Now it was behind them. Now they could move on.

Acceptance is part of working on forgiveness. So is *compassion*. I wanted to teach all the girls to develop compassion toward the ones who hurt them. Compassion is the ability to be concerned for the suffering and misfortunes of others. There is a tenderness in your heart if you're compassionate toward someone. Compassion makes us tolerant and considerate of others. We have a charitable spirit, a big-heartedness toward those who have hit on tough times, for those less fortunate. Compassion has no bad feelings toward the one you need to forgive. On the other hand, it's hard to feel compassionate if you still harbor bad feelings toward the person who hurt you. That's anger still pulling the strings and blocking the ability to be compassionate. Perhaps, you really haven't uncovered all of the sources of your pain. Maybe there's another person who hurt you so deeply the pain is still buried inside, noted Dr. Enright.

Showing warmth and kindness toward the mother who abused you as a little child is no easy thing to do. But if you really want to forgive her and free yourself from the pain that has controlled your life, then you have to realize compassionately that she may have been hurt too. Who knows what she's been through? At any rate, I asked the girls, "Can you see that having you taken away hurt her as much as it did you? Imagine yourself losing your baby to the system. Think of it from your mother's point of view. There's a big piece of your heart being taken away and you are left out, isolated while your baby is being taken care of by a stranger and you don't even know where they live."

Compassion leads to understanding the pain of others and that plays a big role in forgiveness.

Phase 4 -- Releasing the Pain and Anger

    a) Will you take action to release the pain and anger?
    b) Will you take action to communicate with the one
       you need to forgive?

The questions I asked the girls during this phase required them to write down the things that hurt them. Then we took action. The action was a symbolic way of destroying the pain and anger. For example, one girl wrote, "I did not like that my mother agreed with my county social worker to put me on medication for my behavior. My mother really never helped me cope with my anger. She told my social worker that I needed medication to calm me down. Medications were always shoved in my face. If the medications were not working, they'd increase the dosage. If medications were not working, they'd send me to a mental hospital. When I went to visit my mother, we would get into an argument and I would try to fight her, so that's why she wanted me on medications." That was powerful! But once she read this out loud, and everybody heard it, I said, "Burn it."

We burned that note outside on the cement. We assassinated that memory and the pain that went with it. After uncovering the anger, deciding to forgive the ones who hurt, working on forgiveness, now we physically terminated the memory by writing it down and burning the piece of paper on which it was written. Gone. Bye-bye. See you later. Symbolically, we did away with the pain and the anger it produced.

Another girl expressed, "I stayed angry when I was taken away from my mother. I was five years old when I entered the foster care system. I was moved around 17 places. I was diagnosed with ADHD and labeled, so I didn't care what people thought of me. I was abused when I was with a foster family. And no one believed me because I was a child. So I was just an angry child and teenager. And my mother never tried to get me back." After she read it out loud, then I said, "Rip it up!"

She ripped it into small pieces. We took the handful of small pieces outside to the edge of the fence. She threw the pieces high in the air, over the fence and they tumbled in all directions down the slope on the other side. That was that. Extinguished. Knocked off. Finished. The pain was ripped to shreds; the anger was demolished. There was exhilaration in letting those ripped up pieces of pain go flying over the fence. It was soothing, even though it was just a symbol. The symbol represented an action that took place in her mind and in her heart. Ripping up that statement of her anger meant she was in control. Throwing the pieces over the fence meant she was not going to be a victim any more. No more anger, no more pain. Gone. Bye-bye. See you later.

While the last girl cried because she was free, the next girl read her statement, saying, "I struggled with my anger. I was diagnosed with ADHD and I was taking medications for my behavior. Medication did not help me. I still felt angry and depressed most of the time because my mother left me in the foster care system and I missed my family." When she finished saying it out loud, I said, "Shred it."

We went into the office. All the other girls followed. The young lady took her written words about anger and put them through the shredder. It was quick and complete. The anger was sliced into small pieces. Destroyed. Crushed. Put to death. We took the waste paper container with her statement and threw the shredded remains in the large garbage can outside. Let the sanitation man come get it. We were done. Bye-bye. See you later. She cried. We all cried. Taking that action said, "I am free." And we all knew it.

Yet another girl wrote, "I was angry every day. I was angry because my mom put me in the foster care system. I went into group homes because of my behavior. I always felt angry because of my situation. I was 13 when I came into a group home. I was in three different group homes. And I was mad all the time." Shortly after she read it out loud, I said, "Crumple it up!"

She crumpled it up like it was something she truly hated. She squeezed it and twisted it into a little ball of nothing, then opened it up, and crushed it again in her determined hands until it was mangled beyond recognition. "Throw it against the wall," I told her. She did it with enthusiasm. When the smashed ball bounced off the wall and down to her feet, she kicked it back against the wall. There was nothing left when she finished. The paper was smashed and beat up, mutilated, just like her anger and pain. Devastated. Shattered. Trampled. It worked. The pain and anger was finished. Gone. Bye-bye. See   you later.

It was like a sporting event. Every symbol destroying anger and pain was cheered. Every time we put an end to pain and anger was a victory for the individual as well as the group. When another girl mustered the courage to say out loud, "My anger built when I was admitted into group homes. I didn't like being the group homes that locked us up. I didn't like being in group situations with a lot of people. I think that caused my anger to build. When I was angry I cried a lot because I wanted to hit and fight people when I didn't get my way. I'm angry at my mother because she lied to me." "OK," I said, "Bury it!" And that's what she did.

We took the words she had written outside to a dark corner of the property. I handed her a shovel and she started to dig. A little hole or a big hole, it really didn't matter. The idea was clear – "I am going to put this anger and pain underground." She kept on digging, a hole as deep as her calf. And then she put that paper in it. With each shovel of dirt on top of the paper, she felt a release. She said, "It was uplifting to me; I know you may not believe it, but I felt my spirit starting to fly." Well, we did believe it. It had been happening over and over again. Concluded. Defeated. At the end of the line. We buried the statement of her pain and anger and, in doing so, she was set free of the anger and pain. Gone. Bye-bye. See you later.

Another girl articulated, "As soon as I was admitted into the foster care system I became angry. I didn't care. The court system promised me and my sister that we would go home soon and soon never came around. I was promised that I would go home with my mother. That never happened. My anger would continue to build because I was lied too. I didn't trust the foster care system. I hated being labeled and being on medications for my behavior." She stood up and read her statement to the group. When she was done, I said, "Chop it up!"

We took the statement to the kitchen and put it in the blender. The blender roared as it chopped that piece of paper into a thousand tiny pieces. She turned the blender on and off a couple of times to make sure every part of the paper was reduced almost to a fine power. We poured the blended statement into a small bowl and headed to the bathroom. That's where I said, "Flush it!" She put the crumbs in the toilet and pulled the handle. Gone. Bye-bye. See you later. That was the end of that.

This was an exercise that allowed the girls to take action to release their pain and suffering. It may have been symbolic action – only the words were destroyed – but the action meant that they were empowered in their own minds, taking the next step in the forgiveness journey.

Phase 4 is about taking action to release the pain and anger. First, we took action to say out loud what hurts us and then destroy it. Now I asked the girls if they were ready to communicate with the person they wanted to forgive. How can you say, "I forgive you" and "I love you" in different ways? We may not be able to sit down and look someone in the eyes and tell them what we are feeling. I was surprised by what they said.

One girl said, "I am writing a letter to my mom." Her letter captured the "action" of saying something to the one she needed to forgive. It's the step that closes the loop and shows that she had developed to a new level.

Dear Mama, I was thinking about you today after my group session and I wanted to say that I forgive you and love you so much. I miss our family being together. I just want you to get help for your problems. I don't like being away from you and my sisters and brothers. Whenever you decide to get into a drug treatment program, I want to be part of your life again. Mama, I need you and my little sisters and brothers do too. I will write you again next week to check on you.

This letter was a gift in two ways. First, the girl who wrote it was relieved of the burden of anger and uplifted by the beauty of love. Her letter is the language of compassion and forgiveness. She is soft and loving. She misses her family and wants to be together. She is kind and patient – "whenever you decide to get into a drug treatment program..." Second, the mother who received it would definitely be touched by her daughter's growth and tenderness, by her desire to be reunified, and her commitment for the long-term – "I'll write you again next week ..."

The action of communicating with the person you want to forgive is not something superficial. It is the finishing ingredient. Without this important step, the full release of anger and the joy of forgiveness will not be achieved. A second young lady wrote a letter to her mother.

> *Hi, Mama, I learned today to forgive myself. I realized how angry I was at you these past two years for not trying to get me out of the system. But I love and forgive you for the past things that happened to me and you. I hope that you get a good job and make enough money to get a place for us to live. I want to go home now and live with you. I am learning to work on my anger problems and I promise I will try hard not to fight you. I forgive you. Please forgive me.*

For those who didn't think writing a letter was the best way to communicate, other avenues were explored. One girl found a really nice card and sent it to her mother. Another girl bought a coffee mug that had "I love you" on it. Flowers were sent to one mother with a small card that simply said, "I miss you so much." Each gesture became a powerful tool of forgiveness.

One girl verbalized, "I love my mother so much, I just can't trust her. I forgive her. But I know I have to work on me." I said, "Yes, now you're starting to get it! And part of working on you is to take action to let your mother know that you do forgive her. Reaching out to your mother gives you the peace and freedom to work on yourself. Get rid of the pain and anger and watch how you start to feel good about yourself. I've seen it happen. It's amazing!"

She bought her mom a sweet little charm necklace, a mother holding a little baby. We took it to her mother's shelter. On the way, there was anticipation, a spirit of hope. She gave the gift to her mother with a note inside that said, "Mommy, I love you and I really want us to be together." She told her mother to open it after she was gone. She called her later. They cried together.

Every girl said she was willing to forgive her mother but each also said it would be difficult to forget the things that had happened. I said, "You should never forget your life experiences, bad or good, because you can learn from them." When one girl said, "I love my mother. I just wish that she could love me the same way." "Your mother's love is unconditional," I said, "and no matter what has happened, no matter what it feels like right now, she loves you and wishes she could undo the damage she's done. Give her a chance to show her love. It may take time but that love is there and it will come out." She got it.

The moral of this process is that anger destroys lives and forgiveness puts lives back together. There may be pitfalls along the way. For example, a person may decide to forgive, and go through all the phases, but finds that anger emerges again a few months later. This may be an indication that there is hurt and pain from other people that is yet to be uncovered. The hurt and pain might be buried deep inside. Dr. Enright says the process of forgiveness requires that all past hurt and pain be uncovered. If an individual has anger and resentment towards more than one person, the layers of pain must be peeled away one at a time.

Forgiveness is a choice and you have a choice to forgive yourself, your mother, and anyone else who hurt you in order to set yourself free from anger. Forgiving allows people to let go of negative feelings, anger, hatred, resentment, and sadness, noted Richards (1988) (as stated in Enright's book, 1998). The process of forgiving is slow. But one thing is for sure: it's not about holding grudges and getting revenge.

Forgiving softens your heart for the person who hurt you. Think positive about the person who hurt you, and you will develop the compassion to appreciate their shortcomings and their struggles. You can see their weaknesses and understand why they didn't have the ability to prevent your pain. You can still love. The love is your medicine for healing your own heart. There is a truly powerful principal of the Christian faith that teaches this point. No matter how many terrible things we have done, God forgives us. God loves us no matter the mistakes we have made. In this way, the forgiveness approach is our way of implementing God's great plan. Our lives are repaired when we forgive. Our lives are enriched when we love. Our lives are opened up to new people and new experiences when we learn to forgive the ones who brought us hurt and pain. Forgiving will bring you a sense of calmness and peace.

CHAPTER 9

UNCOVERING LAYERS OF ANGER

I developed another way to look at one's anger, to uncover the layers that have built up over the years, fueling the angry behaviors that we all hate to display. In Dr. Enright's method, uncovering anger is the first and most important step. We must have the courage to single out the bad experiences that make us mean and evil toward others. Since pinpointing the source of anger is the essential part of the forgiveness process, I designed a diagram that helps visualize the hurt and pain of years past that lead to anger. Designing this chart helped me identify the ones who hurt me. I call this process *Uncovering Anger One Layer at a Time*. I was able to uncover the traumatic memories of my past and talk about them. I think this will help you, too.

The model on the next page begins at the bottom and identifies the source of anger in my life as I grew up. The chart describes each event that added a layer of anger to my world. These unhealthy layers of anger were stacked on top of one another. It is important for each one of us to identify our own sources of anger. Another person will have different events, different sources, that stimulate an angry reaction. In fact, two people experiencing the same event will have different reactions. For one, the event will be the source of fury and rage. For another, it won't have any notable impact. When I identified the layers that led to my anger, I realized that my siblings experienced the same events and reacted in different ways. Nevertheless, uncovering anger has helped me identify the sources of my outrage. As you do the same, you will find out what it is that has made you angry over these years. The diagram illustrates how the layers of anger were forming inside me.

The graph showing the layers of built up anger. Start from the bottom and work your way up

The 6th layer of anger formed during my painting career when I was called "nigger lover."

The 6th layer of anger

The 5th layer of anger formed when I was getting beat up by the father of my children.

The 5th layer of anger

The 4th layer of anger formed when I got pregnant and dropped out of high school.

The 4th layer of anger

The 3rd layer of anger formed when kids in the community called me "white girl."

The 3rd layer of anger

The 2nd layer of anger formed when my parents divorced.

The 2nd layer of anger

The 1st layer of anger formed when I witnessed my parents fighting.

The 1st layer of anger

The 1st layer identifies where my anger began when I was 10 years old, reacting to my mother and father fighting every Saturday night. These negative memories echoed in my mind and caused me to be stuck on anger. I wasn't old enough to uncover where the anger came from. All I knew was that I was hurt, confused and angry at my parents.

That is when the angry person started to progress inside me. All I remembered was the fighting every Saturday night. As I realize now, this was a disservice to my parents, who were honest, hard-working, dedicated individuals. I was too young to understand the challenges and hardships my parents faced in their early years. All I saw then was the fighting and it made me unhappy and angry. I wanted to do the same things.

I really didn't realize how much the angry person inside me had control. The anger came out at unexpected times. When I thought someone was looking at me up and down, I was ready to fight. Or if I thought someone was talking about me in line at a grocery store, I would stop what I was doing and say, "What the fuck you talking about?" I could be anywhere – at a party with cousins, hanging out in the community park, at the beach with my friends – but if I felt like I was being violated in any kind of way, I was ready to attack and fight. Of course, my anger determine what a violation was. A person may have been thinking, "She's cute," or "She's so nicely dressed," and I would interpret the look through my anger. I could turn a kind thought into fighting words and the person on the other end had no idea what hit them. I had no control over my anger. Looking back, I was blessed I never ended up in Juvenile Hall or in jail for fighting people.

My parents' divorce created the 2nd layer of anger. My parents never talked to me about why they were getting a divorce. I witnessed my dad moving out. I was sad. For many years, I buried that feeling – the feeling of growing up without my father. Now I know it fed my wrath and made me have furious reactions to things. Each layer piled on top of another and the anger boiled inside me ready to explode. I carried the anger around like a loaded pistol. Whenever my father did come to visit, I was happy. I wanted to go with him. But my anger made me so mean and ugly, so much so, he didn't wantto pay much attention to me. No one really wanted me around because of my negative attitudes and behavior. All this did was further fuel my anger. I just wanted to be loved and hugged. I wanted to hear, "I love you, Sylvia." I never did hear that as a child or teenager. I was so angry I may not have been capable of hearing it, even if it had been said.

The 3rd layer of anger shaped when I was a teenager and girls at school called me "a white girl." I lived in the black community and being called a "white girl" was the ultimate insult. I used that insult to trigger my anger and the girl who said it was hit with 110 pounds of outrage. My anger was so righteous and hateful I didn't feel pain if I got hit and definitely no compassion if my victim cried for mercy. My friends were angry, too. Their anger showed in different ways. They may have been afraid to fight like I did, but they were determined to do other things. Many of my friends smoked marijuana daily, sometimes all day and night, hanging-out on the street corners. I was too afraid to use drugs and alcohol. I saw what drinking beer and liquor did to my friends in the community. I refused to be part of that. Even in my early years, I came to realize that I had values and boundaries, things I would do and things I wouldn't do. I loved my friends dearly though I didn't want to do what they were doing. I didn't want that type of lifestyle.

The 4th layer of anger developed due to isolation and fear. I got pregnant at 16 and dropped out of high school. It made me angry that I was separated from my peers. I was even sad because I wasn't in school, though I didn't actually go to school very often and didn't do much when I did. I missed the social environment. At least I could get up in the morning, dress nicely and go off to school like I was a normal kid. Now I was pregnant. It was embarrassing. I didn't know how to put anything in perspective. After all, nobody made me get pregnant. Nobody made me quit school. Nobody made me isolate myself. Yet, all of those things conspired to form another source of anger, another layer to feed my resentment. The pressure of pregnancy scared me. The fear made me mad. There was no one I could talk to about my problems. I hadn't developed any good relationships with adults at school. I couldn't talk to my mother about how I felt; I had to figure things out on my own. At the time, I didn't know why, but the isolation and fear made me nastier and meaner as my anger became the boss of my personality.

The 5th layer of anger occurred when I was 18 years old, living with the father of my two boys. In spite of my isolation and fear, I really thought I was a good girlfriend or "pretend" wife. I cooked dinner every night, kept the house clean, and took care of our babies. My sons' father started coming home late, sometimes he would stay away for two or three days. I refused to accept it. So he started beating me up. One night he beat me with a belt so hard I had welts from head to toe, my body black and blue. I was proud that I walked away and never looked back. Once again, though I was living with anger controlling my life, I realized I had boundaries and limits. I was not going to allow myself to be whipped by a man just because I was in love. Each time I took a positive action to protect my values, a seed was planted that would later grow to give me confidence and self-esteem. I refused to steal. That said something about who I was beneath the anger. I refused to be beaten. That told me that I was somebody, that knew I had value deep down.

The 6th layer of my anger developed when I started working as a painter and my co-workers called me "nigger lover." I was in my early 20's. It hurt so much to hear white people yell ugly names at a black man all the way across the yard, a black man they didn't even know. Nobody took one look at these overweight, uneducated white guys and immediately called them nasty names. It touched a sense of injustice in me. It also fed my anger. I believed for many years that white people were better than me and better than the African-Americans I grew up with. I worked around white males who talked negatively about black people and Mexicans. I honestly believed every white person hated my black friends and me. Because of this, for many years, I struggled in the effort to connect with white people. I put up a wall all around me when it came to having relationships with white people. Anger loves hatred of a whole race of people. That way, anger can be arbitrary and mean without any regrets. This was one major barrier I had to overcome and it was not easy. The sixth layer of built up anger put the ugly icing on the cake. It was very easy for me to get angry at a white person and curse them out.

This method taught me to start from the bottom and peel back each layer at a time. Thinking about what happened enabled me to put my own perspective on the things that made me angry. With perspective, I began to see that there was no reason for me to use anger as a response to each layer. Anger didn't fix anything. A new outlook was the fix I needed.

The uncovering process helped me see that I was trapped in the bondage of anger. For a person like me, who had used anger as a cover-up for so many years, I had to crawl down from my pride. Pride made me defend my anger, as though each layer required the response I had given it. I didn't want to admit that I was wrong, that my anger was unjustified, that I was really no better than the grade school kids who called me "a white girl," or the co-workers who called me "nigger lover." Pride made it hard for me to ask for help. I had to give up my pride, a false pride at that, in order to work on the idea of forgiveness.

I let the pride go, I humbled myself and, finally, I got there. I was happy when I decided to forgive my parents. I had to reflect and understand that my parents did the best they could, raising five children, working several full-time jobs. They had their own problems that probably had not been uncovered or resolved. I began to develop compassion for my parents. I reached out to show them on a daily basis how much I loved them. This helped me to forgive myself for all the things I did to hurt them and other people.

Setting the anger free helped me become a better person inside and out. I stopped worrying about what people said or thought about me. I didn't care if someone looked at me up and down. It didn't bother me that someone was talking about me behind my back or calling me "a white girl." In the process, I learned that the stack of layers made me nastier with people, over almost nothing, because each new layer added another source of rage on top of my original pain and hurt. But once I decided to forgive myself, my parents, my neighborhood friends, and the white people who said nasty things, I released all the layers of anger that had messed up my life.

Dr. Enright's method plus identifying the layers that are the sources of your anger will help you uncover past hurt and pain. This method helped the girls in my care overcome anger issues that hindered their growth and perverted their personalities. After working hard on this process, anger toward their mothers disappeared, allowing them to forgive their mothers and themselves. If I can do it, if my girls can do it, you can do it, too.

Now, begin by writing down your feelings from the first time something happened to you for which you harbor anger. Name the person who did this to you. Proceed to the next layer and continue until you have listed all the people who hurt you and the circumstances that contributed to your anger. Next, ask yourself if you are ready to work on your anger problems. Start talking about your hurt and pain to a close friend, a counselor, a teacher, or a family member. Find somebody you trust who will listen to your story.

After you have identified those who hurt you, then ask yourself if you are ready to forgive them. Ask if you can forgive yourself for the troubles you've caused. Once you have uncovered your frustration and the sources of your anger, ask yourself if you are ready to forgive that person who hurt you. Then ask if you are prepared to start working on forgiveness? Once you have listed on paper what happened that hurt you and the names of the people who hurt you, destroy it, and release it with a symbolic action – like crumbling it up, tossing it in the trash can, grinding it in a shredder. Destroy the paper you wrote on. Let the anger go. Don't let it take control of your life anymore!

Currently, in my life, there are no layers of anger, nothing to uncover or peel back. I refused to remain stuck on anger, to let the anger be my partner in life any longer. I express my feelings immediately. Anger won't have a chance to form in me.

If I start to feel upset about an incident, my feelings are voiced to my husband or friends. A daily journal helps me release my emotions. It's very important to address hurt feelings instantly so no layer develops as a breeding ground for anger.

There are thousands and thousands of people who refuse to believe they have anger problems. Being stuck on anger, many people are numb to the feelings of rage. Anger actually feels normal to them. These people refused to accept responsibilities for their negative behaviors, remaining unhappy so much of the time. Don't let this be you! Uncover the first layer, which could go all the way back to childhood. There are probably stacks and stacks of layers, events that leave scars on your heart and soul. Anger sulks in those layers and develops a hard bitterness toward life. "Are you mad all the time?" "Do little things turn into huge irritations?" "Do you always feel like somebody is doing something to you?" "How far back do you have to go to get at what is hurting you?" These questions will get you going in the right direction if you are honestly ready to uncover the layers that create your anger.

As I mentioned earlier in this book, I was my worst enemy, but I learned that I have the power to control the way I think, the way I behave and what I want to strive for in life. And so do you! The goal is to peel back and uncover your past traumatic events one layer at a time

CHAPTER 10

FAMILY REUNIFACTION

I have learned that family is everything even if we do not like what is happening in our homes. For me, the Saturday nights fights were awful. I didn't understand as a child. Perhaps, if my parents could have sat me down and reassured me that everything was going to be okay, I may have reacted differently. It goes without saying that young parents shouldn't physically fight in front of children. Around small children, verbal abuse and fighting between parents is destructive. Parents are the first teachers and role models. So, please, remember your children are looking up to you for love, guidance, and a safe environment. Arguments and fights are scary and traumatizing. If this happens, I hope you talk to your children, making them feel safe and secure.

I feel honored to have been raised around the black culture most of my life. I truly believe God prepared me for the job He had planned for me. I worked in the group home business with the same type of African American and Hispanic girls I was raised with in my community. Also, the same type of girls I was fighting in school for calling me "white girl" and "bitches."

I enjoyed every minute working with angry troubled foster girls who called me names and cursed at me while I was trying to help them. I recall many saying to me in the heat of the moments, "Fuck you, white lady, fuck you, bitch; you're not my mother, you can't tell me what to do." For 20 years, I heard this kind of talk from many of the teenage girls in my care. But, almost without fail, the next day, or sometimes within hours, they would say, "Sylvia, I'm sorry. I was angry at my roommate and my teacher." I never took the name calling personally. I had learned so much from them that all I could do was hug them and say, "I love you, everything will be okay." These were the best years of my life, teaching the girls to love and forgive their mothers, no matter how much their mothers had hurt them. I will always believe I learned more from my girls than I ever taught them. I learned to forgive my parents. I learned to forgive myself. I learned to manage my anger and love all people no matter the color of their skin.

When my father and mother retired from their primary jobs, I hired both of them to work at the group homes and at apartments I bought to give the girls places to live after they left foster care.

I was excited to be able to see my father and mother throughout the week. The first year on the job my dad drove the girls to and from school every day. After a year he worked as the gardener.

My mother served as a childcare worker in the group homes. The girls called her Grandma. She enjoyed helping the girls with their chores, showing them how to keep their bedrooms clean, wash clothes and cook Mexican food. It was truly a blessing. We spent many lunch hours together talking about family and the work at the group homes. It was beautiful seeing my parents happy and working side by side, as best friends.

In regards to the girls in my care, many were excited about turning 18 and leaving the foster care system. My husband and I had purchased apartments so we could offer the girls housing when they left my care. They had the opportunity to rent studio apartments for $400 a month that included utilities and furnishings. I recall one young lady who aged out of my care and had the chance to live on her own in a studio apartment. Her mother was homeless, pushing around a grocery cart in the community collecting aluminum cans. Instead of this young lady renting the studio apartment for herself, she wanted to live in one of our two bedroom apartments with her mother.

She said, "Sylvia, please help me help my mother get off the streets. I want my mother to live with me in one of your two bedroom apartments." I said, "You'd rather pay market rate rent for a two bedroom than $400 for yourself?" She said, "Yes, I want my mother off the streets. I want her to come and live with me. I'll pay whatever to have my mother live with me." I agreed to help her. The young lady was so happy. We moved her personal belongings into the apartment the day she turned 18. We decorated her home with new beds and furniture. She couldn't believe it was finally going to happen – she was finally going to experience living with her mother. She never had that opportunity before. While sitting on the living couch, crying, she expressed her appreciation, "I will never forget this, Sylvia, I am finally able to live with my mother and see my little brother."

There was another young girl whose mother was going to be released from prison one month after she aged out of the foster care system. She wanted desperately to have a place ready for her mother when she came out. I agreed to help, even though her county social worker wasn't in agreement. This young girl found a full-time job, while completing her high school diploma. When she turned 18, she moved into her apartment. A month later her mother was released from prison and moved in with her daughter. The mother enrolled in a drug treatment program and found a part-time job. The young girl said, "My mother can finally braid my hair and we can spend quality time together. I am so happy! Thank you, Sylvia, this is a dream come true."

I understood how much these young girls wanted to be with their mothers and family members. They dreamt of opportunities like this. These young lives changed the moment I said, "Yes, I'll help you get things organized so that you and your mother can live together."

One day my younger brother, David, a sanitation supervisor who lays tile on the side, was laying ceramic flooring in the group home. I drove up the driveway that Saturday afternoon to see how the flooring was coming along. I saw my nephews outside cutting tiles. One was about 17 and the other 19 years old. I sat in the car and I watched them for a few minutes. At that moment, I came to the realization that I hardly knew my nephews. My anger had robbed me of the chance to know my brother's family. If I didn't like something about his wife, I cursed her out. If I heard that she said something about me – whether she did or didn't – I would say the type of ugly things that would make anybody in his life want to stay away from me!

I was so busy living mad, waiting for the next opportunity to express my bitter resentment, I never made the effort to get to know my nephews in a personal way or spend quality time with them. Watching them on that Saturday brought tears to my eyes – living examples of what I had allowed anger to take away from me. Anger makes you throw valuable precious time down a rat hole. That day reinforced my notion of the importance of family.

I moved out of my home when I was 17 years old and really never had the chance to get to know my little brother, David, or my big brother, Oscar, as a young adult. My little sister, Rachel, worked at the group home, so I saw her every day. My sister, Hortencia and I really never got to know each other as young adults.

She and I eventually became very close when she was diagnosed with ovarian cancer. We were both in our late 40s. I cared for my sister for eight months while she went through chemotherapy. She lived with me. We shaved our heads together. Eleven months apart in age, we got to know each other very well as middle-aged adults. What a different experience. When we were children and teenagers, I beat her up and called her names. She was a victim of my anger. When she faced cancer, I cared for her – cooked for her, fed her, gave her baths. I was her voice and protector when she couldn't speak to doctors.

We got to know each other on a deep personal and spiritual level, like sisters should. I read her my journals written over 20 years. We shared secrets. We laughed, cried, and prayed together. We went to the movies and church on the days she felt good. We did everything together during those eight months. The point here is that, in our early years, my righteous anger made me huff and puff around like a suicide bomber, ready to blow everything up at the slightest irritation. No one wanted to say anything to me, much less share an intimate feeling or observation. In our younger years, there I was with my anger, like an alcoholic with a bottle, isolated, in a dark corner, cut off from my sister. Back then, she could hear the tick, tick, tick of the time bomb of anger that followed me around everywhere I went. In the end, my personal growth and her unfortunate cancer brought us together as never before.

It's been five years since she went home to be with God. I truly miss her and regret not really knowing her during our youth and adult years. I was angry and mean to her when I was a teenager. We ended up living our separate lives in the same town as we became adults. It breaks my heart to think about it, because it was primarily my fault. I have come to realize family is everything to me. Family should be everything to you, as well. Love your siblings, mothers and fathers, no matter what. Forgive them, and yourself, for what happened in the past. Don't wait until you or someone in your family gets ill and is ready to die. Make time for your parents and family members now. Love them unconditionally.

As I grew as a person, as I purged myself of the anger that had dampened my spirit, I wanted my family in my life. Understanding this, I empathized with my girls and made every effort to make sure they had every chance to see their mothers and family members. One day, I drove across town to collect rents from several of my tenants and I had two of the girls in my care with me. As I approached the apartment complex I owned, one of the girls said, "I remember this neighborhood. My grandmother lives in the next few blocks over there," she said, pointing in the direction she wanted me to go. We drove that way, then she added, "It's that small blue house on a corner." I said, "Okay, I will drive over there and park and we'll go knock on the front door and ask for your grandma." She said, "I've not seen my grandma, sister, mother, or father for 7 years."

We pulled over, got out of the car, and I knocked on the front black screen door. The grandma, a little short four-foot Mexican woman with dark brown hair, came to the front and looked through the screen. As the grandma opened the door, I saw the grandfather sitting on the sofa. They must have been in their late 80s. The girl said, "Hi, grandma, it's me." They hugged. The grandma turned her head and called out a name – her little sister – to come to the front door. The little sister jumped on her big sister, hugging her tightly. They both cried. The grandma cried. I cried. The grandma told me in Spanish why the teenage girl was not with her family. The parents were in prison.

The teenage girl was so happy. She said "I am going to take pictures of my grandma, grandpa, and my little sister to show my friends at school and my socialworker."

That same night the teenage girl sent the pictures to her county social worker from her iPhone. The next morning, a very upset social worker called me. She said, "Sylvia, I can't believe you allowed this to happen without the court's approval." The social worker was on a roll, chastising me for several minutes. I listened but, deep down, I cried. She had no idea what this experience did for that teenager. Seeing her family changed her attitudes and behavior from that point on. She had not seen her family in 7 years! Prior to this encounter, she was one of the worst girls in my care. Her tantrums were legendary. She was out of control, with anger problems off the charts, refusing to obey any rule in the home. She tested every limit and all boundaries. After that short, thirty minute visit, supervised by me, an officer of the court, that girl was never the same. All she talked about was turning 18 so she could go back home to live with her family.

After that unexpected encounter, she went to the next court hearing and told the judge the story of her chance meeting with her family. On the spot, the judge approved visitations with her grandmother. It was beautiful to see the young girl's reaction when she saw her family. It brought tears to everybody's eyes. After 7 years!

There was another beautiful moment when a young lady in my care connected with her family. It all started when there was a community Heritage Parade in which the girls and I participated. I drove my black convertible with the hood down, loudly playing Kirk Franklin's song, "Stomp," while the girls danced alongside the car. They had their dance steps down tight, performing in the street. We won second place.

At the end of the Parade, while we were eating lunch, a woman with three children walked up to us. Seeing the woman, one of the girls jumped up, saying, "That's my big sister. I haven't seen her since I was a little girl." The young women said to me, "We have the same father." To her little sister, she said, "When I saw you dancing in the street, I knew that was you with those long legs. It's been 6 years." She added, "You know our father lives here in San Diego."

The teenage girl in my care didn't think she had any family members living in San Diego. She was happy that day to meet with her big sister. And, believe me, happiness was never a term used to describe this girl. She was the one mad at everyone and everything. She was the one no wanted around. During Thanksgiving and Christmas, she was alone. She was vicious and mean toward everybody, had a miserable attitude, a lousy outlook, and was always ready to attack with anger. The next business day, I notified the county social worker that we had met this young girl's big sister. A few weeks later the teenage girl started day visits with her big sister and eventually met her father.

Family reunification changed her entire outlook on life. When she met her sister, I saw a change in her cold indifference for the first time, like when the sun meets ice. She smiled now, felt connected to somebody important to her. She hadn't seen any of her family members since she was a little girl. Nothing made me happier than to see this transformation.

My life has come so far that Saturday nights are no longer something I worry about.

Saturday nights are different now.

I spend some of my Saturday nights going to dinner with my mother. Some Saturday nights, we go to the beauty salon to get our hair colored and our nails done. On Saturday nights, my father visits me now. Saturday nights are good nights. I have my mom, my dad and my family. No more fighting, no more arguing, no more anger.

This is what family is all about, about those times when mothers and fathers starts preparing Thanksgiving feasts, two days beforehand. A time when the house starts smelling like turkey, ham, dressing, pumpkin and sweet potato pies. It's a time when the family sits together around the table to eat, laugh, and be thankful for all the blessings received throughout the year. It's a time for everyone to be happy. A time to reflect on the good times, as people connected together forever.

Family is Christmas. A time to shop for a Christmas tree and decorate it with the kids, while Mama makes hot cocoa. It's a time when all the lights in the home are turned off to better see the Christmas tree light up. A time to buy gifts. A time for giving and sharing. A time for feeling the well wishes of your family members as you open up gifts that represent kind thoughts and warm relationships. A time for celebrating the meaning of Christmas. A time to reflect on the good times, as people connected forever.

Family is the Easter holiday. A time to go to church as a family. A time to hide Easter eggs so the children can run around the yard looking for them. A time for mothers and fathers to cook and barbeque. A time to celebrate the renewal and miracle of life.

Family is celebrating birthdays and family reunions. Special times for sharing, laughing, crying and supporting one another in times of joy, in times of need and suffering.

There are millions of teenagers and young adults who are angry at their mothers, fathers, sisters, brothers, grandmas, aunts or uncles. If you're one of them, don't cheat yourselves out of the chance to be with your family. Don't miss out on the sharing that makes memories to last a lifetime. You can overcome the anger that separates you from all the things you love the most.

I have written this book from the bottom of my heart to share with you the importance of uncovering anger in your life one layer at a time. For some, including me, anger was explosive, something that could go off at any time. For others, anger is a slow burning disorder that puts a miserable dark cloud over everything in life. Whether a ticking time bomb or a constant gloom, anger is working hard to make us unhappy, depressed, and lonely. I am an example of the fact that it doesn't have to be that way. Don't let the anger exist in the dark shadows. Take the cover off. Identify the hurt and pain. Forgive your mother, father, and whomever hurt you. Forgive yourself for the ugly things you did in the past. Reach out to your family and friends. They need you and you need them.

Anger is a crippling ailment that corrupts lives if it's not uncovered and addressed. You have the power to control your thoughts and behaviors, you have the power to release the pain, and you have the power to forgive. Make the decision today to forgive the ones who hurt you! Set yourself free! That's the power of forgiveness. Take it from me. I am living proof!

Bibliography Index

The bibliography represents my attempt to gather additional readings and research that relate to the topics of this book, including, but not limited to, anger, forgiveness, forgiveness education, foster youth, and the latter's struggles while living in group homes during their teenage years.

Additional bibliographic entries are drawn from the County of San Diego's foster care system, as well as articles detailing the issues surrounding foster youth as they transition out of the foster care system. The bibliographic list underscores the themes and challenges identified in this book and provide a road map for further reading and exploration.

Bibliography

Administration on children, youth, and families programs (2011).
Health and human services. Retrieved from
www.acf.hhs.gov/programs/acyf.

Allen, B. & Vacca, S. J. (2010). Frequent moving has a
negative affect on the school achievement of foster
children makes the case for reform. *Children and youth
services review 32*, 829-832.
doi:10.1016/j.childyouth.2010.02001.

Aldridge, J., Goldman, R (2007). *Current issues and trends in education*
(2nd edition). Sage

Annie E. Casey Foundation (2004). Theory of change: A practical
tool for action, result and learning. Organization Research
Services. Retrieved fromwww.organizationalresearch.com.

Berzin, S. C. (2010). Understanding foster youth outcomes: Is
propensity scoring better than traditional methods? *20.*
doi:10.1177/1049731509331873. Retrieved from
http://rsw.sagepub.com/.

Bennett, S. D., Sullivan, W. M., & Lewis, M. (2010).
Neglected children, shame-proneness, and depressive
symptoms. *Child Maltreatment, 15*, 305-325 doi:
10.1177/1077559510379634. Retrieved from
http://rsw.sagepub.com/.

Blake, S.C., & Hamrin, V. (2007). Current approaches to the
assessment and management of anger and aggression in
youth. *Journal of Child and Adolescent Psychiatric Nursing,
10*, 209- 221.

Bruskas, D. (2008). Children in foster care: A Vulnerable
    population at risk. *Journal of child and adolescent psychiatric
    nursing 21. (2)*, 7- 70.

Burns, W. J., Quartana, J. P., & Bruehl, S. (2008). Anger
    inhibition and pain: Conceptualization, evidence
    and new directions. *Journal of Behavioral Medicine
    Springer Science + Business Media,* LLC. doi:
    10:1007/s10865-008-9154-

California Health and Human Services (2007). Foster youth
    services: California welfare Services. Retrieved from
    www.chhs.ca.gov/.

Candelaria, M.A., Fedewa, L.A., & Ahn, S. (2012). The
    effects of anger management on children's social
    and emotional outcomes: A meta-analysis. *School
    Psychology International, 33,* 596-614. doi:
    10.1177/01430343124543060.

Casey Family Foundations (2007). Education children in foster care.
    The McKinney-Vento and no Child Left
    Behind Acts. Retrieved from www.casey.org.

Casey Family Foundations (2011). The promoting safe
    and stable families program. Retrieved from
    www.casey.org.

Chamberlain, P., Leve, D. L. & Smith, K. D. (2006).
    Preventing behavior problems and health-risking
    behaviors in girls in foster care. *International Journal
    of Behavioral and Consultation Therapy, 2,* 4-

141

Deffenbacker, L. J., Oetting, R. E., Lynch, S. R., & Morris, C. D. (1996). The expression of anger and its consequences. *Elsevier Science Ltd, 34* (7) 575-590. Department of psychology, Colorado, State University, Fort Collins, Co 80823. S0005-7967(96)00018-6

Dowdell, E. B., Cavanaugh, D. J., Burgess, A.W. & Prentky, R. A. (2009). Girls in foster care: A vulnerable and high-risk group. *The American Journal of Maternal Child Nursing, 34*, 172-178. doi:10.1097/01.NMC.0000351705.43384.2a.

Dreher, N. (2003). Anger: It can be frightening. *Journal Current Heath, 29*, 20-24. Retrieved from http://ehis.ebscohost.com/eds/delivery.

Farruggia, S. J. & Sorkin, D. H. (2009). Health risks for older U.S. adolescents in foster care: The significance of important others' health behaviors on youths' health and health behavior. *Child: care, Health & Development, 35,*340-348.

Enright, D. R. (2012). *The forgiving life: A pathway to overcoming and creating a legacy of love.* American Psychological Association. Washington, DC.

Enright, D. R. (2011). *Forgiveness is a choice: A step-by-step process resolving anger and restoring hope.* American Psychological Association. Washington, DC.

Enright, Robert D.; Fitzgibbons, Richard P. (2000). *Helping clients forgive: An empirical guide for resolving anger and restoring hope.* Washington, DC, US: American Psychological Association.

Enright, D., North, J. (1998). *Exploring forgiving* The University of Wisconsin Press, Madison Wisconsin

Galvez, (2015). *A Phenomenological study of ex-foster care Hispanic and American women's perception during secondary education* (Doctoral dissertation). Retrieved from Pro Quest University of Phoenix Library.

Galambos, L. N., Barker, T. E. & Krahn, J. H. (2006). Depression, self-esteem, and anger in emerging adulthood: Seven-year trajectories. *Development Psychology, 42*, 350-365. doi: 101037/0012-1649.42.2.350.

Fehr, R. Michele, J. G. & Nag, M. (2010). The road to forgiveness: Review of Psychological Bulletin, 136, 894-914.

Finch, J. R. (2006). Trauma and forgiveness: A Spiritual inquiry. *Journal of Spiritual in Mental Health, 9*, 341-355. doi: 10.1300/J515v09n02-0

Fives, J, C., Kong, G., Fuller, R. J., DiGiuseppe. (2010). Anger, *aggression, and irrational beliefs in adolescents.* Albert Ellis Institute, 45 East 65 Street, New York, NY 100069, USA. 33,199-208. doi: 10.1007/s10608-009-9293-3.

Haghighi, B. & Lopez, A. (2012). Success/failure of group homes treatment program for juveniles. Federal probation, 00149128, 93 (57) 3. Retrieved from http//ehis.ebscohost.com/eds/detail/sid=5f9340d0-6d79-49a7-ac...

Hains, A. (1989). An anger-control intervention with aggression delinquent youths. Department of education psychology, P.O. Box 413, University of Wisconsin-Milwaukee, Wisconsin 53201. *Behavioral Residential Treatment, 4,* 166-190. John Wiley & Sons.

Havlicek, J. (2011). Live in motion: A review of former foster youth in the context of their experiences in the child welfare system. *Children and Youth Services Review 33.*1090-1100. doi:10.1016/j.childyouth.2011.02.007.

Iglehart, P. A. & Becerra, M. R.(2002). Hispanic and African American youth: Life after foster care emancipation. *Journal of Ethnic & Cultural Diversity in Social Worker.* The Hawthorne Press, Inc.

Jackson, J., Kuppens, P., Sheeber, B. L., & Allen, B. N.(2011). Expression of Anger in Depressed Adolescents: The role of the family Environment. *The Journal of Abnormal Child Psychology 39,* 463-474. doi: 10.1007/s10802- 010-9473-3.

Jackson, J. L., O'Brien, K., & Pecora, J. P. (n.d.). Posttraumatic stress disorder among foster care alumni: The role of race, gender, and foster care context. *Journal Child Welfare, 90,* 5-10.

James, S. (2004). Why do foster care placement disrupt? An I investigation of reasons for placement change in foster care. *Social Service review.* University of Chicago. doi: 0037- 7961/2004/7804-000.

ee, H. S., Conn, M.A., Szilagy, G. P., Blumkin, A., Baldwin, D. C. &
Szilagy, M. A. (2010). Identification of social-emotional problems
among young children in foster care. *The Journal
of child psychology and psychiatry 51:12,* 1351-1358.
doi: 10.1111/j.1469-7610.2010.02315.x.

ohnson, J. A., Musial, D. Hall. E. G. Gollnick, M. D. & Dupuis, L.
V. (2008). *Current issues and trends in education. Foundation
of American education: Perspective on education in a changing world*
14th ed.). Boston, MA: Pearson Education.

err, A. M. & Schneider, H. B. (2008). Anger express in children
and adolescents: A review of the empirical literature. *Clinical
Psychology Review,* 28, 559-557. doi:10.1016/j.cpr.2007.08.001.

andsverk, J. A., Burns, B. J., Reutz (2009). Psychosocial interview for children
and adolescents in foster care: Review of research literature. *Journals
Child Welfare league of American, Inc.* 88. 49-69. Retrieved from
http://search. Proquest.com.ezproxy.apollplibrary.com/213807053.

awrence, V. (1978). *The seven deadly sins today.* University of
Note Dame Press. Notre Dame, London.

MacLeod, J. & Nelson, G. (2000). Programs for the promotion
of family wellness and the prevention of child
maltreatment: a meta-analytic review. *Journal of child abuse
and neglect, 24* (9), 1127-1149. Doi: 10.1016/so145-2134
(00)00178-2.

Mayne, J. T. & Ambrose, K. T. (1999). Research review on anger in psychotherapy. *Journal of Clinical Psychology, 55,* 353-363. doi: 10.1002/ (SICI) 1097-4679(199903).

McDonald, P.T., Allen, I. R., Westerfelt. & Piliavin, I. (2002). Assessing the long- term effect of foster care: A research synthesis. What happens after foster care? A new investigation. *Social Service Review.* Retrieved from www.child**welfare**.com/book/references.htm

Meichenbaum, D. (2006). *Comparison aggression in boys and girls: A case for gender-specific interventions.* Retrieved from University of Waterloo Department of Psychology.

Mullins, D. & Tisak, S.M. (2006). Moral, conventional, and personal rules: The perspective of foster youth. *Journal of Applied Development Psychology 27,* 310-325.

National Casey Alumni (2003). Assessing the effect of foster care- Indiana. Retrieved from www.inpathways.net/casey-alimni- studies.

O'Connor, S. (2001). Orphan trains: *The story of Charles Loring Brace and the children he saved and failed:* University of Chicago press.

Oswald, H. S., Heil, K. & Goldbeck, L. (2010). History of maltreatment and mental health problems in foster children: A review of the literature. *Journal of Pediatric Psychology, 35,* 462-472. Oxford University Press.

Osvat, C. (2012). Children in need. Predisposing facts in preventing child abandonment and school dropout. *Sociology & Social Work Review*. Retrieved from msw.usc.edu/Social-Work- School. Polirom Publishing House.

Philpot, C. (2006*). Intergroup apologies and forgiveness*. University of Queensland, Brisbane, Australia. American Psychological Association Occasion of The 59th Annual DIP/NGO Conference United nation Head Quarters Midday Workshop.

Quartana, J. P. & Burns, W. J. (2007). *Painful consequences of anger suppression*. Department of Psychological Association. University of Miami, Coral Gables, FL.7, 400-414. doi:10.1007/s10865- 007-9127-2.

Quartana, J. P., Yoon, L. K., & Burns, W. J. (2007). Anger suppression, ironic processes and pain. *Journal of behavioral Medicine, 30*, 455-469. doi:10.1007/s10865-007-9127-2.

Racusin, R., Maerlender, A. C., Sengupta, A., Isquith, P. K., & Straus, M. B. (2005). Community psychiatric practice: Psychosocial treatment of children on foster care: A review. *Community Mental Health Journal, 41*, 2- 9. doi: 10.1007/s10597-005-2656-7.

Rees, A., Pithouse, A. (2008). The intimate world of strangers- embodying the child in foster care. *Journal of Child and family Social Work, 13*, 338-347. doi: 10.1111/j.1365- 2206.2008.00558.x.

Reid, J. M. Emery, R. C., Drake, B. & Stahischmidt, J. M(2010). Understanding chronically reported families. *Child Maltreatment, 15*, 271-277. doi:10.1177/1077559510380738.

Reifsteck, J. (2005). Failure and success in foster care programs. *North American Journal of Psychology*, 7, 313-326. NAJP. Ruffolo, M., Sarri, R. C., & Goodkind, S. (2004). Study of delinquent, diverted and high-risk adolescent females: Implications for mental health prevention and intervention. *Social Work Research*, *28*, 237-245.

Ryzin, V, M, & Leve, D. L. (2011). Validity evidence for the security scale as a measure of perceived attachment security in adolescent. *Journal of Adolescence.* doi:10.1016/adolescence.

San Diego, Community Care Licensing Division (2014). Retrieved from ccld.ca.gov

San Diego, Health and Human Services (2010). Retrieved from www.sdcounty.ca.gove/hhsa.

San Diego County Demographics profile (2011). Retrieved from www.sandiego.gov/planning/profilies/southeasternsd

Santrock, W. J. (2009). *Life-Span Development* (12th ed.). McGraw-Hill.

Senn, E, T. & Carey. M. (2010). Child maltreatment and women's adult sexual risk behavior: Childhood sexual abuse as a unique risk factor. *Child Maltreatment*, 15, 324-335. doi: 10.1177/1077559510381112.

Sharkin, S. B. (1996). Understanding anger: Comment on Deffenbacher, Oetting, et al., (1996), Deffenbacher, lynch, et al., (1996), and Kopper and Epperson (1996). *Journal of Counseling Psychological* 43,166-169.

Smith, K. D., Stormshak, E., Chamberlain, P., & Whaley, B. R. (2001). Placement disruption in treatment foster care. *Journal of Emotional and Behavior Disorder,* *9*,200-205.

tone, S. (2007). Child maltreatment, out-of-home placement and academic vulnerability: A fifteen-year review of evidence and future directions. *Children and Youth services Review 29*, 139-161.

Strijker, J., Knorth, E.J., Knot-Dickscheit, J. (2008). Placement history of foster children: A study of placement history and outcomes in long-term family foster care. *Journal of Social Services and Child Welfare, Psychology, Sociology, Medical Sciences, 87*,107-124.

Stuart Foundation (2013). Retrieved from www.stuartfoundation.org/.../at-greater-risk-California- foster-youth-and-the-path.

Turner, G. M. (2008). *Treatment foster care for improving outcomes in children and young people.* The Cochrane Collaboration. John Wiley & Sons.

Tyler, R. W. (1949). *Basic principles of curriculum and instruction.* University of Chicago Press.

Unrau, A. Y., Font, A. S. & Rawals, G. (2012). Readiness for college engagement among students who have aged out of foster care. *Children and Youth services Review, 34*, 76-83. doi:10.1016/j.childyouth.2011.09002.

U.S. Department of Health and Human Services (2003). *The AFCARS Report: Preliminary FY 2011 Estimate as of 2010.*

U.S. Department of Health and Human Services (2012). *The AFCARS Report: Preliminary FY 2011 Estimate as of 2011.* Foster care data snapshot. *Child trends 19,* 1-7.

U.S. Department of Health and Human Services (2012). Retrieved from www.hhs.gov.com

Usher, L. C., Randolph, A. K. & Gogan, C. H. (1999). Placement patterns in foster care. *Social Service review.* The University of Chicago.

Vacca, S. J. (2008). Breaking the cycle of academic failure for foster youth children-What can the schools do to help? *Journal of Children and Youth Services Review, 30,* 1081-1087. doi: 10.1016/j. childyouth.

Vecchio, D. T., O'Leary, D. K. (2004). Effectiveness of anger treatment for specific anger problems: A meta-analytic review. *Journal of Clinical Psychology Review 24*(1) 15-34 doi: 1016/j.cpr.2003.09.006

Ward, A. (2006). Models of 'ordinary' and 'special' daily living: matching residential care to the mental-health needs of looked after children. *Child and Family social work.* doi: 10.1111/j. 1365-2206-2006.00423.

Ward, S. F. (2012). Boys & girls together? *The Journal of ABC 98,* (12), 17-18.Retrieved from http://search.proquest.com.ezproxy.apollolibray.com/docvie w/1…

Whiting, J. B. & Lee, R. III. (2003). Voice from the system: A qualitative study of foster children's stories. *Journal of Family Relations, 52,*288-300.

Whiting, D. & Bryant, A. R. (2007). Role of appraisal in expressed anger after trauma. *Journal of Clinical Psychologist, 11,* 33-36. doi: 10.1080/13284200601178136.

Williams, A. C. (2011). Mentoring and social skills training: Ensuring better outcomes for youth in foster care, *Child Welfare League of American 90,* (1) 59-74.

Worthington, L.E. (2005). *Handbook of Forgiveness*. Routledge New York. Hove Yen, I.H., Hammond, W. & Kushel (2009). From homeless to hopeless and health less? The health impact of housing challenges among former foster youth transitioning to adulthood in California. Department of Medicine, University of Californian, San Francisco.

Zetlin, G. A., Weinberg, L. A. & Kimm, C. (2005). Helping social workers address the educational needs of foster care. *Child Abuse & Neglect, 29*, 811-823. doi: 10.1016/j.chiabu.2004.12.009. Pergamon.

Zetlin, G. A. & Weinberg, L.A. (2004). Understanding the plight of foster youth and improving their educational opportunities. *Child Abuse & Neglect*, 28, 917-923. doi:10.1016/j.chiabu.2004.03.010. Pergamon.

ABOUT THE AUTHOR

Dr. Sylvia Galvez has 20 years' experience working with troubled teenagers and young adults who struggled with anger. She has dictated her life to serving foster girls, 13-19 years old. She is the owner and licensee of Sullivan's Group Homes, a non-profit organization in San Diego, California, now called Galvez Community Services.

Currently, Sylvia teaches life skills, anger managementand a forgiveness approach to help people uncover their hurt and pain.

Sylvia believes in the power of forgiveness. Sylvia grew up in the inner city of San Diego, California, an angry child who would rather fight than learn. She was pregnant at 16, a high school dropout; by 21, a single mother with three boys. She returned to school at 28, and has never stopped learning. Dr. Sylvia Galvez is married and has 15 grandchildren. She loves the Lord God, almighty!

Appendixes A

Phase 1 -- Uncovering Anger

c) Who are you angry at?

d) Are you ready to work on your angerproblems?

Phase 2 -- Deciding to Forgive.

a) Can you identify the ones who hurtyou?

b) Are you ready to forgive them?

a) Are you ready to forgiveyourself?

Phase 3 -- Working on Forgiveness

a) Are you ready to work on acceptance?

b) Are you ready to work oncompassion?

Phase 4 -- Releasing the Pain and Anger

a) Will you take action to release the pain and anger?

b) Will you take action to communicate with the one you need to forgive?

Appendixes B

Six layers of anger uncovered!

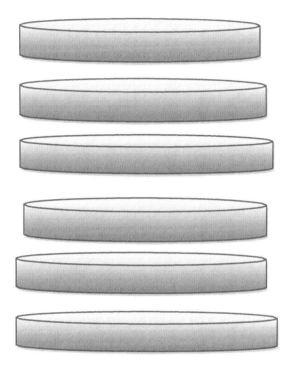

Uncovering Anger One Layer at a Time

Dr. Sylvia Galvez

Made in the USA
Las Vegas, NV
05 November 2023

80292188R00087